FEAR INTO ANGER

Py Bateman

FEAR INTO ANGER

A Manual of Self-Defense for Women

Photographs: Larry Seide

NELSON-HALL CHICAGO

Library of Congress Cataloging in Publication Data

Bateman, Py.
    Fear into anger.

    1. Self-defense for women.   I. Title.
GV1111.5.B37 1978   796.8'1   77-19122
ISBN 0-88229-441-5 *(cloth)*
ISBN 0-88229-603-5 *(paper)*

10 9 8 7 6 5 4 3 2 1

To my instructor and my students, who in their own ways, gave me the tools and the impetus to develop the knowledge that is the basis of this book.

Contents

Preface

That our contemporary society is extremely violent is a fact hammered home to us in daily reports from radio, television, and newspapers. Violence is deeply ingrained in our society. It is a sociolegal problem that will take many generations to eradicate. Despite the considerable attention focused on violence in the past years, the situation is still not improving. Crime rates are on the rise everywhere. Every day, crime touches more lives. We cannot afford to wait for a fundamental change in society. We must learn to defend ourselves against violence right now.

A violent tragedy may well happen to you and your family. You may think such a thing cannot happen to you, only to other people, but if you wait until violence *does* strike to think of prevention, you will be too late. It is better to think now about prevention, before anything happens.

The material in this book is like knowledge of first aid. You master it, all the while hoping that you will never have to use it. On the other hand, learning the material means you will be able to respond if the necessity ever arises. Read each chapter carefully and practice the techniques you learn. The directions and explanations are written clearly and simply.

Women of all ages should read this book. It is equally important to housewives and working women. A copy should be kept in every American household. As girls grow into women, they should be given this book to read and study. I think this book will give you confidence—in your mind and your body.

Chuzo Kotaka, 8th dan, Shito-ryu karate
Founder and president, International Karate Federation
AAU national director of Shito-ryu karate

Introduction

I have been teaching women karate and self-defense for more than five years. During that time I have learned more about women and self-defense than I thought there was to learn. This book is, in a way, the crystallization of my teaching experiences and the development of my ideas and techniques of self-defense.

When I first began teaching women, I tried to give them a portion of my training in traditional Japanese karate—the portion that had been taught to me as "women's self-defense." I taught the type of techniques that fill many of the books on self-defense written by men in the 1950s and 60s. The moves were specialized reactions to various offensive moves. I noticed that when my students worked on such techniques in pairs, they had considerable difficulty. Yet the problem was not in the technique itself. Problems arose when the offensive member of a pair made a mistake like stepping in on the wrong foot or using the wrong hand. The defensive partner was unable to correctly apply the technique.

After watching my students struggle with "women's self-defense" for a while, I decided that the best thing to do was to teach them to fight. I began to give them a more traditional and well-rounded program of karate. I emphasized sparring (free fighting), so that they would learn to react to the unknown. I taught them that the first task in an assault situation is for one to take control of oneself—as soon as a woman perceives herself to be in danger, she should start fighting.

I still believe that knowing how to fight is the best way to defend yourself. Anyone who has to wait for an assailant to make a move must then respond to what he is doing, which means operating at an unnecessary disadvantage. You cannot learn how to fight from a book. If you are interested in learning, read the chapter on karate and find a good school.

Knowing how to fight is still a limited approach to self-defense. Even a skilled fighter can be surprised and caught in a hold in some circumstances. This book will get you started and will be a good supplement to your formal training. However, not all women can afford the time or money for formal courses in karate. Furthermore, many have no inclination toward such intensive training.

The techniques presented in this book are designed to give the untrained woman as complete a program as she can derive from informal training, as well as to supplement formal training that does not deal directly with self-defense. They are simple and direct techniques, and they are effective. They are meant to be used by women who need them, not to dazzle readers or impress other karate instructors.

The most important skill that I hope you will gain from this book is not physical, but mental. The techniques presented here are only tools. They are not pat answers to specific circumstances of attack. If you are ever attacked, you will have to make decisions. I hope that you will study this book in such a way that you will automatically think effective defense. Study the principles behind each technique; come to understand why they work in the way they do.

The possible variations of specific assaults on women are incredibly numerous. Every time I speak in public on the subject of self-defense, people in the audience ask me, "What do you do if. . . .?" My own students frequently ask, "What do you do if. . . .?" Over the years, I have developed the ability to decide quickly what would be the best reaction. You must do this for yourself. As you read this book, ask yourself over and over, "What would I do if. . . .?" Find as many answers as you can based on the principles you learn.

The problems throughout the various chapters are exercises in making choices. Look first at the attack. Make up your own response before you look at the solution I present, which is, after all, only one possible solution among many. Study the solutions and discover the thought processes behind them— the choices that were made. Make up your own problems; teach yourself to think quickly and decisively. You will find no guaranteed techniques in this book and, of course, every attack varies, and probably none would be identical to a situation in this book. Still, every technique is simple and effective—you are given enough information so that you will be able to know when to use it.

I am grateful to all those who helped me in their many different ways. I owe a special debt to those who made my stay in Honolulu more comfortable when I was first beginning: Linda McCrery and Ira Rohter for their hospitality; Rita Howard and Sandra Holmes for their interest and for reading some of the first drafts. I am also indebted to my instructor, Chuzo Kotaka, who gave me some good ideas and encouraged me to pursue the book to its finish, and to Karen Reischel, women's athletic trainer at the University of Washington, who read the manuscript and gave good suggestions for improving the chapter on exercise. My students in Seattle acted as guinea pigs to test my written instructions with patience and enthusiasm. And I am especially grateful to Suzanne Mitten, Lauri Moss, Ellen Punyon, Kathy Reid, Terri Saporta, and Sue Williams for the time they took to model for the photographs, and to Bob Bragg and students from Roger Tung's Northwest Chuin Yin Whai Martial Arts Association for their willingness to play villain in the photographs. And I thank Robert, whose unbounded enthusiasm and confidence in me pushed me to keep going when things got rough.

Chapter 1

The Prevention of Rape

American women are looking for a new solution to an age-old problem. A profound fear of sexual assault has been handed down from mother to daughter for generations. Our fear is not imaginary; it reflects a real situation that is intolerable. Throughout our collective memory our sex has been subject to unprovoked and unpredictable sexual assault —assault that is always brutal and sometimes fatal.

The impact of rape reaches much further than to its victims and their families and friends. Rape terrorizes the entire population of women. The secrecy in which sexual assault has been shrouded, the shame connected with rape in our culture, and the random choice of victims by rapists have contributed to the terrorization of women everywhere. The fear has become a part of our everyday life, always lurking just beneath the surface of our consciousness. It surfaces when we hear of a woman in our neighborhood who was raped or when a spectacular case receives a lot of publicity.

I remember my first encounter with the knowledge that I, because I am a woman, am in danger. It was my first year at college. Early in the summer two young women disappeared. During a long search for them and after their bodies had been found, when another search for their killer was mounted, ten-

sion turned to near hysteria in the town. Other assaults on women that would normally have been reported in the back pages of the newspapers were moved to the front pages. Self-defense classes were offered at the Y. Advice was offered from all sides to the terrified women students.

For many nights I lay in bed listening to the creaking of the building or the rubbing of a tree limb against a window. Walking on campus after dark, I tried to keep away from the bushes, where I imagined vicious men to be lurking. When I was alone, I was afraid something would happen, and there would be no one to help me. If I saw a man in the same area, I was afraid he might be the killer.

You may be surprised to find out that this was not the time I took up karate as a means of learning self-defense. To the contrary. The bodies were found, and the killer was caught. The town and I gradually pulled away from the extreme edge of fear. The self-defense classes and the advice disappeared. The rape stories returned to the back pages of the newspaper, and I returned to my carefree way of life. Still the fear never completely went away; I had just found a way to live with it.

It was not until I took up karate and learned to take care of myself that I

1

lost my fear. Only in losing it did I realize that it had been with me for so long. In separating myself from fear, I realized that self-defense is more than a way to protect oneself from potential sexual assault. It is a way of improving all our lives by freeing us from the lurking fear that has become so much a part of us.

American society is shocked and outraged by spectacular accounts of brutal rapes, but the American way of life supports the fear in which women live as a result of such outrage. Rape has always been recognized as a problem in our culture. The solutions that have been advanced, however, have delicately (and at times not so delicately) skirted around one area—the idea that women could take care of themselves. Attempts to control sexual assault have ignored the need for a fundamental change in men and women. They have preserved the image of women as passive beings who, if not protected by someone else, have no choice but to submit to whatever assaults men choose to force on them. Traditionally, we have been promised protection by our fathers and husbands, and by the representatives of the state, the police departments.

Women who lack male protectors are somehow suspect if they are raped. Surely they have been provocative and somehow deserve what they have gotten. And women whose male protectors fail to protect them shoulder the burden of guilt that men refuse to accept. How many men have said to their raped wives, "How could you do this to *me*?"

We find ourselves in a double bind. We are told, on the one hand, that we cannot resist men who are physically so much more powerful than we are. We rely on our protectors, the knights on white horses who have greater success in dreams and legends than in reality. When they fail, we are at fault. It's no wonder that our biggest defense—in our own minds at least—is denial. Rape simply can't happen to us.

When we hear of a woman who has been raped, our denial is shaken. In order to reestablish the idea that "it can't happen to me," we look for the differences between ourselves and the victims. It is this search for differences, I believe, that has suckered women into participation in the myth that a rape victim deserves what she got. If we believe that rape victims provoke assault by their dress or their manner, then we can believe that *we* are safe because we don't provoke assault. We live in the right neighborhoods, dress conservatively, avoid contact with strange men—and passionately believe that it could never happen to us.

And when it does happen, as it often does, the myth of the guilty victim backfires, turning against us. Many victims believe themselves to be guilty just because they have bought the idea that all rape victims are guilty. In addition to all the physical and psychological pain that goes along with rape, these women must cope with their undeserved feelings of guilt.

The truth is that no woman provokes rape. Any reasonable person looking objectively at the situations and circumstances of numerous rapes should be able to see that. Women have been raped in all kinds of neighborhoods, dressed in a wide variety of outfits, by strange men and by friends and relatives. We have been raped on the streets and in parks, and in our own homes. We have been dragged sleeping from our beds to be raped by men who have broken into our houses. While some of us are perhaps more attractive asleep than others, I don't know any woman who while asleep in her bed can allure a man passing by on the street.

Some may accuse me of oversimplification, but I firmly believe that the idea of provoked rape is nonsense. Even a woman who "teases" (another concept I don't believe in), dresses alluringly, or flirts with strange men is not inviting assault. She may be inviting sexual experience or adventure—but on her own terms. Rape is not a sexual experience; it is a suffering of violence, often brutal violence.

Rape is the only violent crime in which our society even remotely entertains the idea that the victim could possibly invite attack. No one accuses banks of provoking robbery just because they obviously have a lot of money around and hand it out to some people willingly. And our societal sanctions against murder are so strong that no matter how sincerely and explicitly a person asks to be killed, anyone who complied would be prosecuted. Yet because our society confuses the violence and brutality of rape with sexual desire, the idea persists that a woman can provoke assault.

Defeating this idea of a victim's guilt is one of the first steps in changing the image of women from that of perfect victims to self-sufficient, self-respecting human beings. There is no way that a woman can defend herself properly if she is not sure that she has the right to do so. We should feel immediate indignation when approached by an assailant; instead, our reactions often reflect bewilderment, confusion, and guilt. We must be convinced that we have the right to our own integrity and its defense. There is nothing that gives a man the right to invade the body of a woman—neither his physical strength, nor the woman's dress, nor her appearance or actions, nor her lack of a protector.

Differences in physical strength between men and women and the resulting fear of serious, lasting damage or death, has been seen as the reason that women should submit to male assaults, defending ourselves only by seeking protection from "safe" men. Not only are we advised that we will be unsuccessful in a physical contest with a man, but we are warned of the dire consequences of trying. The supposition that a woman who fights back against a rapist will only make him angrier and more likely to kill her is based on the assumption that the woman's struggles will be ineffectual. I have seen a filmed interview with a convicted rapist who said that if a woman tried to struggle against him, he would kill her. He believes that because he sees women as weak and passive. Yet a rapist who is disabled by his victim will not be able to retaliate, much less kill her.

Our society tends to view women as weak and passive. A rapist seeks a victim who embodies that image. He relies so much on finding one that often even a small show of aggression on a woman's part sends him scurrying off to look for easier prey. Too often, though, he's successful in finding a "good victim," because most women to some extent see themselves as weak and passive. Weakness and passivity are qualities that are carefully bred into women. Many of our experiences as we grow up support and confirm the weak and passive image. Even when girls are at an age when they play vigorous games, they are reminded that men are superior to them.

Remember the old go-ahead-honey-hit-me-in-the-stomach game? A big, strong man offers his stomach to a small girl, demonstrating that men are invulnerable to the blows of a woman. I have yet to hear of a man saying, "Go ahead, honey, kick me in the groin." From hitting your father (uncle, brother, cousin) in his tensed stomach to wrestling with your teen-aged boyfriend, your playful experiences frequently point toward the physical superiority of men—and to their invulnerability to women.

The media goes a step further in exaggerating the differences. Television and films abound with violence; these media depict men as almost supernatural, able to endure incredible physical stress. Women, on the other hand, are shown as weak, especially when faced with a violent man. One man may hit another, knock him down two flights of stairs onto a street where he is run into by a car. The injured man will, of course, jump up to pursue his torturer. A woman who is struck by a man usually dies, or at least ends up in the hospital. Viewers who have no experience to the contrary end up with the impression that men are very tough and women are extremely frail.

The truth lies somewhere in between. More important than the strength differential between men and women is the fact that the human body is funda-

mentally strong. Women, as well as men, can take quite a bit of physical punishment and still function adequately. It takes a lot of care and determination to disable a human being, male or female. Women have an advantage over men in determination, since we are defending ourselves. Furthermore, we do not underestimate them. We expect them to be strong, so we attack their weakest points.

A small woman should not cringe at the thought of having to defend herself against a large man. She should make her body as strong as it can be and use her strongest techniques against the weakest parts of his body. Once women get rid of the idea that men are all-powerful and we are too weak to resist, we can deal with the problem of how to use our strength to the best advantage. Until we are convinced that we have some kind of chance of coming out ahead in a physical encounter, however, we will never try. The first prerequisite to fighting back is the will to defend yourself. No one can give you that; it is something you have to develop for yourself. The will to defend requires self-respect and confidence. You must believe that you are worth fighting for. And you must believe that you have a chance to succeed.

The development of maximum strength is so important to self-defense that chapter 8 is devoted to physical conditioning. Strength is important, not only for proper execution of the techniques taught in this book, but for self-confidence. Development of strength, and the feeling of being in tune with one's body that comes with it, creates the basis for confidence.

Confidence itself is a crucial aspect of self-defense. Men who prey on women frequently are looking for a specific type. They want someone who is easily frightened and submissive. Experienced rapists who are adept at picking out victims especially seek this type.

Women, on the other hand, have been trained to fit the role of the perfect victim. Our reactions to the petty assaults that are common in our lives—whistles, cat calls, uninvited touches—are but miniversions of the ideal (from the point of view of the rapist) reaction to rape. Almost universally we react with fear, embarrassment, and a desire to get out of the situation before anyone perceives that something is going on. In doing so, we take the burden of guilt on ourselves. Our reaction also shows our fear that the petty assault will lead to something more serious and dangerous. Such intrusions function to train us to be victims.

Today women are beginning to change this scenario. More and more women are responding with self-respect, indignation, and anger, but such reactions are hard to maintain without some degree of self-confidence and the physical ability to back up the response.

Looking at recent police statistics, I was amazed at the percentage of rapists who gained access to their victims' homes through unlocked doors and windows. Lack of basic precautions is another thing that often brings rapists and victims together. I have long maintained the opinion that we, the victims, should not be required to curtail our lives because they, the offenders, attempt to molest us. I resent the idea that a woman should stay at home after 8 P.M. in order to avoid the violence that might be committed against her just because of her sex. On the other hand, I think that common sense can guide a self-confident woman to take precautions that do not detract from the quality of her life, but do protect her privacy from intrusion.

Women have been bombarded for years with ideas for safety precautions that we should take; they range from staying home after dark to looking in the back seat of our cars before we get inside. Women lead different lives, and each woman must tailor her safety precautions to suit her life and needs. I find it exasperating that every list of safety tips I've ever seen assumes that all women live alone and work in the daytime, in a city. These things are no more true of all rape victims or potential rape victims than they are of all women. Each of the various aspects of women's lives has an impact on our vulnerability to assault and on our ability to prevent or defend against assault.

The first step toward taking safety precautions is to examine your own life-style and patterns. Find out where you are most vulnerable. Note the conditions that you would have to take into account in the event of a struggle or flight. A good example of one aspect of women's lives that is often ignored in the realm of self-defense is the presence of children. With children present, everything changes, from the security measures you take in your home to the manner in which you would fight back if attacked. This is only one example of the different conditions of women's lives that make safety and self-defense a very individual matter.

Self-defense is also a different matter for those who live in groups. In the past ten years there have been several notable cases in which one or two men have been able to terrorize a group of people who outnumbered them. One of the most spectacular involved one man who held eight women captive, and killed seven of them one by one. One woman saved her own life by hiding under a bed.

Groups of people who are menaced by a smaller number need unity in order to defend themselves. People who live in groups should discuss self-defense among themselves. When faced with an intruder or intruders, the first person to move against them needs to know that the others will back her up. The more coordinated a group is, the more successful it will be in defending against intrusion.

A careful examination of your life-style helps you to determine possible options of defense. Fighting back is not always the best answer. In some circumstances running away, bargaining, fast-talking, and other ploys are best. Examining your daily routine will enable you to put together a working plan for the sort of response you would give to various possible attacks. Don't dwell on the possibilities of assault to the point of paranoia, but take a week or so to look at your life in terms of self-defense. Determine where and when you are most vulnerable to assault and what responses would be appropriate under what conditions. Thinking about such things ahead of time gives you the ability to react quickly and surely in the event of an actual attack.

Another individual aspect of self-defense is your values. Women are subject to a variety of assaults that range from purse-snatching to rape and murder. No one can tell you how far you should go in defending your purse or your life. That is something each woman has to decide for herself. Every situation in which self-defense is a possible response entails a certain amount of risk to everyone involved. There is risk in the assault itself and a risk in fighting back. Every person and every situation is different. It is impossible to predict every possible situation, but you can lay down some guidelines for yourself.

Consider various degrees of assault, taking into account what you stand to lose in each type of encounter. Consider how much risk is involved in each situation. Then make some preliminary decisions about your responses to different combinations. Just like the examination of your life-style, setting guidelines now will help you respond quickly if the need arises. Set limits for yourself as to how far you would go in complying with an assailant who had a big advantage over you in power. Set some guidelines for your response to weapons. You may decide that an assailant can take your purse, but not your camera. You may decide that you would take off your clothes, but you won't let anyone tie you up. (Setting these guidelines will come more easily after you have finished this book.)

Rapists frequently move in on their victims gradually. They intrude just so far, and if they are successful, they push a little further. A victim often doesn't perceive what is happening until it is too late. You need constantly to be alert and wary. And you must respond in such a way that you put an end to the intrusion before he takes control of the situation.

Each woman must construct a personal program of rape prevention that fits her life-style and her values. No expert can tell you what to do, but this book does describe a basic program that you can fill out according to your needs. A good program of rape prevention consists of four interrelated parts. First, develop your strength to its full potential. Second, take precautions that will make you an unlikely candidate for victimization. Third, know your own values and set your own limits. To achieve these three things you need confidence and self-respect, the connecting fibers that hold a personal program for rape prevention together. Confidence and self-respect are necessary to achieve the first three parts of the program. These qualities you must make for yourself. The fourth part of the program, knowledge, you can get from this book.

Even the knowledge gained from this book, however, requires some input from you. I will give you the tools, but you must use your own mind to fit this knowledge into your individual rape prevention program. I could have taken the easy way in writing and provided you clearly defined responses for various types of attacks, but this would be contrary to my philosophy of self-defense, which is based on the fact that each individual is different and must create her own solutions. You must put more effort into this program of self-defense, but you will get more out of it. You will be able to replace your fear with self-respect, and you will find yourself angered at intrusions upon that self-respect. You will be able to anticipate, avoid, or defend yourself against a wide variety of assault situations. I believe in women's abilities, and I have confidence that you will be able to learn—and adapt as your own—the techniques in this book.

Chapter 2
Counterattacks

Passive self-defense is a luxury a woman cannot afford. It is vitally important to put a speedy and definitive end to any attack. It is not enough to escape a hold if an attacker stays around to grab you again.

Your defense should be measured against the strength and determination of the attack and against your opportunity for escape. You must stop an attacker decisively, satisfying yourself that he is no longer a threat.

Each situation dictates a particular defense. Too often women have been told: "You don't need to study self-defense. Just run away." In some circumstances, running away is a good thing, even for a highly trained woman, but for a woman isolated from help, it might not be the best alternative. And running away from a potential rapist is impossible under some circumstances, such as when you have children present.

Sometimes simply running away, a yell, or slipping out of a hold is enough to secure your safety. In many situations, you will have to move even more aggressively in order to stop the assault. This chapter gives you the tools for aggressive self-defense. Study the techniques and learn them well. Practice regularly according to the program presented at the end of the chapter.

Vital Targets

Where you hit an assailant is almost as important as whether you hit him. Many men believe themselves invulnerable to a woman's blows. They probably have never been struck by a woman, except maybe on the arm or chest. The popular media image of a woman beating her fists helplessly against a strong man's chest has had its effect on all of us.

Some parts of the body are able to withstand more force than others. After all, Tarzan beats his *own* chest. It is to the weakest areas of the attacker's body that your blows will have the best effect. Study chart 1, which shows the vital targets. Mentally prepare yourself to immediately attack any of these areas.

Some areas are so tender that an effective blow to one of them can often stop an attack completely. Some areas are also susceptible to permanent or serious injury, so you will have to decide whether the assault warrants such a defense.

Eyes can be attacked by poking with the fingers or some object. At a minimum, this will cause an assailant considerable pain and difficulty in

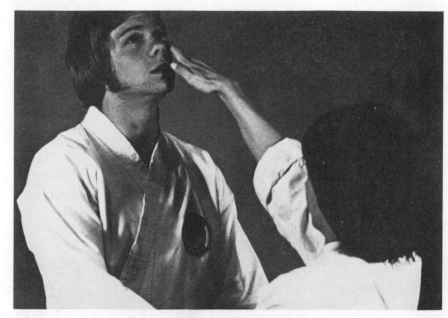

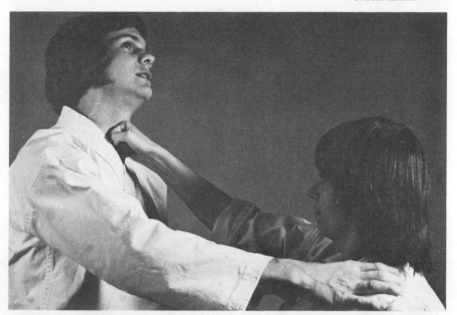

seeing. Some tissue damage may occur, but you don't have to worry about eye-balls popping out or anything else very melodramatic. Most women shy away from attacking the eyes out of squeamishness. Don't hesitate. You need not at-tack both eyes. One will usually be enough, and aiming at just one is easier. If the assailant is wearing glasses, move your hand up forcefully under them.

Strike at the throat. A strong blow to the throat with either the fist or the outside edge of the palm of your hand causes temporary constriction of the breathing mechanism. A man who is having difficulty breathing will not give much attention to you as you escape or continue your defense. A great amount of force could cause a collapse of the trachea, a serious injury that can lead to suffocation. Although such an injury is possible, it is not probable that you would cause it accidentally. Students in my classes have occasionally received accidental blows to the throat without sustaining permanent injury. The danger of permanent injury is slight enough to make the risk worthwhile. Once you have delivered such a blow, escape. When the attacker began his assault, he gave up his right to consideration from his intended victim.

Pressing on the throat with an open hand helps push away someone who is very close to you. As soon as you gain more space, you will probably want to adopt a more vigorous technique. Pressing or grabbing and twisting the

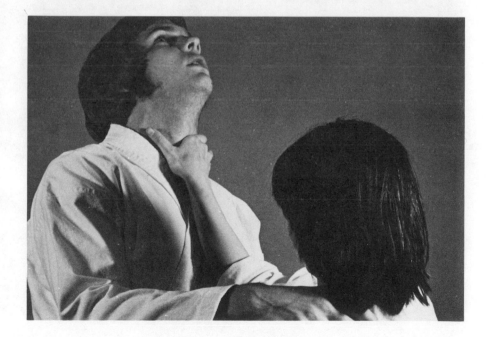

Adam's apple are good techniques for situations in which you have been thrown to the ground or surprised in bed.

The groin is a very tender area in men, vulnerable to a variety of defenses. You can use your hands to punch, grab, and twist. You can kick with a foot or knee. Some men respond to a threat by quickly protecting the groin area, so, if you combine a blow to the groin with one to the throat or some other tender spot, your assailant's attention will probably go to the groin, leaving the other target unguarded.

While a blow to the groin is painful, it does not necessarily inhibit a determined attacker. The best defense is a series of three or four blows, rather than a single one. Aim for the testicles, coming up from underneath.

Kicking the knee is another good defense, especially against a tall assailant whose head may be out of your effective reach. Without a functioning knee, it is difficult even to stand up and often impossible to walk or run. The knee can be hit from just about any direction with good results. A blow from the side may sprain or dislocate the knee. A direct blow from the front will damage the kneecap, fracturing or dislocating it. Force directed against the back of the knee causes buckling and temporary loss of balance. There is usually no pain or injury involved with a blow to the back of the knee.

The shin is the front part of the leg below the knee. It is bone, covered with little more than a layer of skin, which makes it extremely tender when struck. A blow to the shin is not usually disabling, but it may put an attacker in an uncomfortable and awkward position while you continue your defense.

These targets are vulnerable, but they are not magic knock-out points. Blows must be delivered with as much force as you can muster and with perseverance. Don't kick an assailant in the knee and stand back expecting him to

fall down in agony. Continue your defense until you are sure he can't continue his attack or until you can safely escape.

Ironically, these vital areas are often ones that many women are too squeamish to go for. Indeed, such vulnerable targets are usually taboo in a "gentleman's fight." But remember that men who attack women are not looking for a fair fight. If women are to successfully defend themselves, we must make up our minds to use all our strength against their weakest points. You are justified in throwing out all the rules in your own defense—it may save your life.

Your choice of targets, however, cannot be determined simply by vulnerability. A number of other factors enter into your choice. There are times when you will have to aim for less vulnerable targets, because of the assailant's position in relation to you, or some other variation in the circumstances. When your defense is directed to the less vulnerable areas, you will require more force and a sustained series of blows to stop your assailant effectively. Such targets are most valuable in situations in which you are trying to maneuver into a position to use another technique or in a situation where you judge that a minimum of resistance will be enough to end the episode.

Vulnerable spots on the head include the temple, jaw, ears, nose, mouth, chin, eyes, and the back and side of the neck. A blow to the ear (or even better, both ears simultaneously) may affect equilibrium, making an attacker dizzy and unable to continue. The area around the eyes and nose is quite sensitive to pain. One consequence of a blow to the eye is swelling and closing, but this process usually takes more time than you want to spend in such company.

The nose and mouth bleed easily on most people. Even though a bloody nose doesn't usually cause much pain, there is often a panicked reaction to the blood and difficulty in breathing. An assailant with a bloody nose usually reacts by attending to his nose. Because this reaction is psychological rather than a reaction to physical pain, you would do well in most cases to kick the attacker in the groin while he has his hands to his nose or mouth. The psychological shock won't last very long, so don't hesitate and lose your opportunity to continue.

A blow to the chin has an adverse effect on balance. If you are going for a knock-out, the chin is the best target. Coupled with the painful effects of these blows to the head, is the psychological shock most men feel at being struck in the face by a woman.

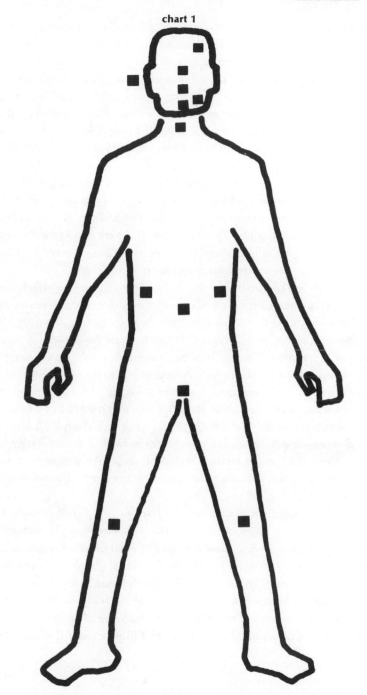

chart 1

chart 2

Regardless of what you have seen on television, people do not drop unconscious to the floor when struck on the side or back of the neck. Direct your defense to the neck only when better targets are out of reach.

There are times when the torso is the only target area presented to you. If you have any choice at all, avoid directing your defense to that area, since it is well-protected. If a blow to the torso becomes absolutely necessary, the most vulnerable spots are the solar plexus and the floating ribs. The ribs on the right side protect internal organs and are more susceptible to pain and injury than the ones on the left.

The solar plexus is a nerve center located just behind the point at the lower end of the sternum where the ribs come together in an inverted *V*. If you press hard on your own solar plexus, you can feel a slight discomfort that can be magnified many times by a forceful blow. If it took you more than two seconds to find your own solar plexus, however, think how it will be looking for that exact spot on somebody who is trying to strangle you.

It is taboo in the American concept of fair fighting to attack someone whose back is turned. Certain circumstances may demand, however, that you use the back as a target, and besides, there is nothing fair about this kind of fight. If an assailant's back is turned to you because he is running away, you may choose to let him go. But he may be running down the hall to your sister's room, or he may have turned to pick up some rope to tie you. If you hesitate in taking advantage of his weakness, you may make an effective defense harder. In such circumstances direct your blows with as much force as you can muster to the most vulnerable spots, the kidneys and spine (see chart 2). It is often possible to direct your defense to the groin from behind if the attacker's legs are far apart. Since the back is well-protected, if you strike a blow at it, you will have to continue your defense when the attacker turns around to find out what's happening.

Defending yourself is always an uncertain prospect, full of variables and unknowns. You must learn to size up the situation quickly and carefully, weighing the advantages and disadvantages of each possible response on your part, and decide what to do. The information in this book gives you the tools needed to put together an adequate defense for most of the situations you might encounter. The construction of your defense, if and when you ever need it, however, is up to you. Throughout the following chapters are problems; sample situations of assault. Study these techniques carefully, and then use

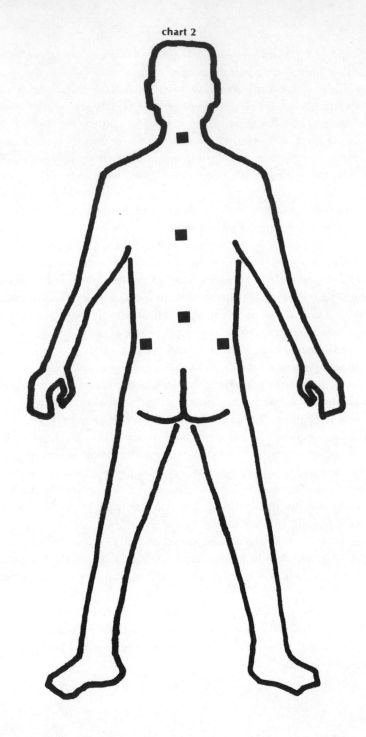

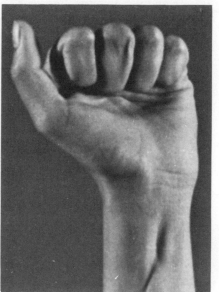

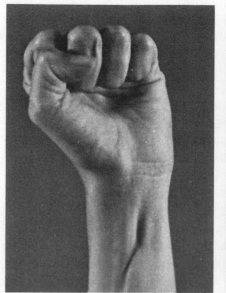

your own imagination to consider other possible situations. As you study the counterattacks in this chapter, think back to the vital targets. Carefully consider each possible combination of counterattack and target; then weigh the positive and negative points of each.

Punch

The most versatile hand technique in self-defense is the basic karate punch. It is designed to maximize your power, and deliver it efficiently and quickly to your target. A punch can be directed to practically any target on an attacker's body, and it can be used from a variety of positions and distances.

Since our hands were developed for more delicate tasks than punching would-be rapists, the karate punch is also good because it gives maximum protection to your hand.

Learn to make a proper fist, so it can act more efficiently as a weapon and so your hand can return more readily to more pleasant functions. To do this, open your hand, stretching your palm and keeping your fingers together. Curl your fingers as tightly as you can, rolling them into your palm. Place your thumb, as illustrated, outside your fingers, supporting the first two fingers of your fist. The knuckles of these first two fingers should be the principal focus of your fist; they are the strongest. Long fingernails will hamper the formation of a good fist, so you will have to decide which is more important to you.

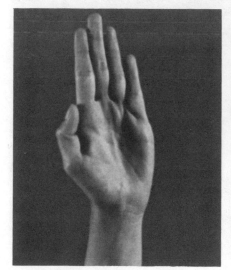

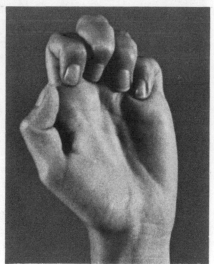

In addition to protecting your hand, correct karate form gives protection to your wrist. In all phases of the punch, the wrist should be held so straight that a pen placed on it lies flat. This is not a natural position for most people, so you will probably have to watch your wrist carefully for a time, until you develop the ability to feel its position.

In practicing the basic punch, stand erect and comfortably with your feet about shoulder's width apart. Keep your head up and your eyes straight ahead. Make a good fist with each hand, curling your fingers tightly.

To begin, place your left hand in front of you, with the palm of your fist facing down and your wrist straight. Imagine that your first two knuckles are touching the solar plexus of a potential assailant. Your right fist is at your right side, palm up. Your right arm from elbow to fist is straight and parallel to the floor. Your shoulders are relaxed, and your right fist is lightly touching your rib cage. Hold the right elbow tightly toward your spine.

To execute a punch with the right hand, extend the fist out to the front, your arm rubbing along your rib cage. At the same time, start pulling your left fist in to your left side, once again staying close to your own rib cage. The two

fists pass each other closely, right in front of your solar plexus. They are traveling at about the same speed and in almost the same path.

As your right fist approaches the limits of its reach, turn your wrist so the palm faces down as your arm extends fully. At the same time the left fist is coming in to the rib cage, it also turns and the palm now faces up. This turning of the right wrist just before reaching target gives your punch snap and penetrating power.

As you practice, your body should be relaxed. Just at the moment your fists are reaching their destinations and turning, tense both fists, arms, and finally your whole body. This is the imaginary moment of impact; the tensing is called snap or focus in karate. Relaxation-tension alternation is an efficient method of utilizing power, as well as a technique to keep you from tiring too quickly. The principle involved in focus is the same as in breaking a string. To

break a string, you do not stretch it tightly between your hands and put steady, forceful pressure on it. Instead, you hold it lightly, slack, and then suddenly you tense, pulling it forcefully apart and snapping it in two. The same principle applies in karate.

Practice your punch slowly at first; then do it faster and with more power as you become increasingly comfortable with the movement. Practice is a continual necessity, partly because you will have a few points that you will almost constantly have to correct. Remember to keep your wrist straight at all times. You will probably feel an increasing tenseness in your neck and shoulders; try to keep your shoulders relaxed. There should be a minimum of movement in your shoulders; don't throw your shoulder into your punch because it will upset your balance.

As you grow more comfortable with the punch, experiment with your

aim. Go back to the section on vital targets and practice punching, aiming for various points on the body. Use a friend for a dummy—touching only lightly, of course. If you are studying this book with a friend or a group of friends, you have a good opportunity to practice with one another.

If you want to get a feeling of how hard you can punch, don't use your friends. Try a pillow or a cushion. If you have access to a health club or similar facilities, try some of the punching bags there. Punching bags are often designed for use with boxing gloves, so you may want to wear some soft padding on your hands. Special equipment for practicing is available from martial arts supply houses.

Try punching from various positions. In a real situation you will not have time to set up an ideal practicing pose. As you go about your daily tasks, imagine how you would punch someone from each different position.

Kiai

As you practice, add a fierce and angry yell to your punches. The karate yell, or *kiai* (key-eye), which comes from your diaphragm, is strong and loud. Each person develops her own *kiai*.

Although there is a surprise element in the yell that may throw an opponent off guard, there are no magic words that will cause an assailant to immediately drop to the floor. Freezing action is one of the main purposes of the *kiai*. A sudden loud noise will shock anyone into inaction, at least for a moment. Your *kiai* should be sudden, forceful, and loud enough to make even the most determined attacker hesitate. It should express anger rather than fear and should let an attacker know he is not going to get the passive response he's looking for.

As you practice punching and yelling, you will notice that you are able to punch harder when you *kiai*. This gain in strength is not an illusion. As a result of physical and psychological forces, any technique is stronger when combined with a *kiai*. The explanation is too detailed to go into here. Just plan to use your *kiai* when you're under attack—you'll need all the help you can get.

Since it comes from the diaphragm, the *kiai* is more explosive than a scream from the throat and lungs, and it is less likely to be affected by the common fear response that constricts the trachea. Many people are unable to make a sound at all in frightening situations, and some people experience difficulty in breathing. The explosion of air coming out of your throat will help to clear the constriction.

The forceful expulsion of air in the *kiai*, in addition to increasing your strength, will also enable your body to better withstand the shock of any blows you might receive. If you perceive that you are going to be hit and you can't do anything about it, *kiai*. Not only will it decrease the effect of the blow when it makes contact, but it may startle an assailant to such an extent that he will not be able to follow through on the blow.

The *kiai* is by far the most useful and versatile technique you will learn from this book. It can be used in every conceivable situation—except maybe under water. A violent encounter between a man and a woman is more than just a physical confrontation. It is a test of wills, of spirit. Even if an attacker's body is bigger and stronger than yours, your mind—your determination to defend yourself—can be stronger than his desire to dominate and humiliate you.

In many ways the *kiai* is the connection between your mind and your body. It communicates on a primitive level. The anger you feel at the intrusion of an attacker is expressed to your body as well as to him, and your body responds with increased vigor and strength. Once you break his spirit, defeating him physically will be easy.

It is often difficult for women to develop a good strong *kiai*. We have been trained to speak in quiet, moderate voices and avoid forceful displays of anger. Women are frequently embarrassed by first attempts to *kiai*. Still, the importance of practice cannot be stressed too much. You must become comfortable with the *kiai* and make it into a reflex. You must automatically respond to danger with your *kiai* and your will to defend yourself. Practice your *kiai* as you practice other techniques. Experiment with different sounds; test the effect of the *kiai* on your performance of other techniques. Once you get used to it, you will probably find that it is great fun.

Front Kick

Karate employs a variety of kicks, using different parts of the foot as a weapon and delivering power in different directions. Often it is the variations of kicks that sustain interest in the matches of sport karate. They are quite beautiful and breathtakingly exciting.

For the woman who is trying to learn as quickly as possible to protect herself, the front kick is the most practical. A front kick is fairly easy to learn from a book, although it takes considerably more practice than the punch. It is very strong, since the power flows in a straight line. Although good balance is necessary, the lack of rotary motion in this kick keeps the need for concentrating on balance at a minimum.

The kick can be directed to a variety of targets. The most effective targets are the groin and the stomach. Kicks aimed at these targets are hip level kicks that have the double advantage of great power and the ability to extend over a great distance.

Distance is one of the assets of the kick. You can hold an attacker at such a distance that he cannot reach you with his hands. Once your kick travels upward, though, the distance between you and him decreases and you lose the advantage of distance. You may regain the advantage if you are able to kick high enough to hit his head.

For now we shall concentrate on the hip-level kick. As you master this technique, experiment with higher kicks, but do not be seduced by what you see in the movies. Remember that what you gain in flash and target, you lose in strength, distance, and balance.

Once you have mastered the classical karate front kick, there are some variations according to shoes, dress, and target. Work on mastering the correct form because, no matter what variation you end up using, perfection of form will enhance your effectiveness.

In order to remove balance as a factor at first, there are two phases in which to learn front kick. In the first phase you won't have to worry about your balance; in the second you will gain balancing abilities that will enable you to deliver more power with your kick.

Phase I

Stand relaxed with your shoulders against a wall. Don't worry about your back touching the wall at all points. Position your feet a shoulder's width apart so they support your weight evenly and comfortably. Your heels will probably not touch the wall, but keep both heels on the floor at all times. Your hands should hang down at your sides, or hold them at chest height in front of you. Clench your fists if that helps, but avoid unnecessary tensing of the upper part of your body. Your head should be up, your eyes looking straight forward.

First practice the kick in four parts. Alternate legs, so one doesn't get over-tired and both get practice. Begin with the left.

1. Lift your right knee straight in front of you. It points at

the spot you want to kick. For a hip-level kick, your thigh is parallel to the floor. The right foot is close to the left knee. The right ankle is flexed 90 degrees so the sole of the foot is parallel to the floor. The left knee is slightly bent. Your back is straight; your head is up.

2. Extend your right leg straight in front of you. If you cannot straighten your knee, you will need to exercise to stretch out your hamstrings (back thigh muscles) and strengthen your quadriceps (front thigh muscles) (see chapter 8). Extend your right ankle in a straight line until the sole of your foot is almost parallel to the floor. Curl your toes toward you so the ball of your foot can be used as the weapon. The extension of the ankle is difficult to master, but it is important to the kick. If you have trouble, try the four steps of

the kick while sitting on the floor. In the sitting position you can more easily concentrate on the ankle movement.

3. Return to the same position as described in Step 1. The withdrawal is important to your balance as well as to protect your foot from being grabbed. It has the extra advantage of returning you to a position from which you can kick again, if necessary.

4. Set your foot down, returning to your original position. You are now ready to kick with the left foot.

Practicing in these four steps familiarizes you with the details of correct form, but 1–2–3–4 kick is not such a good thing when you're faced with an actual assailant. As soon as you feel comfortable with the four steps, progress to performing all four in one smooth motion.

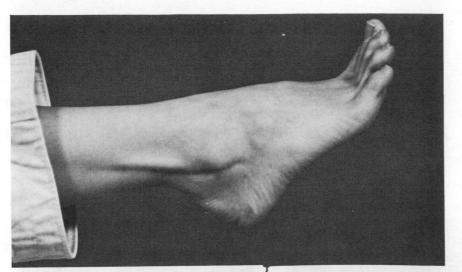

Kick straight in front of you. Each time your foot should hit the same target spot. Keep your body erect and relaxed. As with the punch, tense your body, especially your foot and leg, at the moment of impact. As this motion becomes easier for you, move away from the wall and practice holding your own balance. Holding your leg extended in Step 2 as long as you can is a good exercise for your kicking muscles.

Phase II

In Phase II, a different stance is used. Put your left foot two-and-a-half to three feet in front of your right foot. (The position may be shortened or enlarged depending upon your size.) For stability, separate your feet by about a shoulder's width. Both knees are bent, the front one at an angle of about 100 degrees and the back one only slightly. Your weight is distributed evenly; your heels remain flat on the floor. Your front foot points directly to the front; the back foot is turned out about 30 degrees.

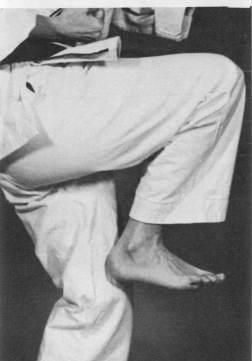

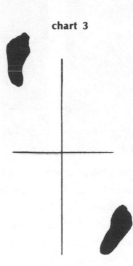

chart 3

Your left arm is held comfortably in front of you with the elbow bent at 90 degrees and held in front of your rib cage. The palm of your left fist faces your body in front of your shoulder at about the same level. Your right hand is held as a fist close to your right side, as if ready to punch. This fighting stance can be used with almost all techniques. As you learn new techniques, refer back to this section and try them out in fighting stance.

From this position you can kick with your right foot by following the same four steps as in Phase I. Lift your knee, extend your leg, return to the bent-knee position, and then set your right foot down behind you in the original position. For kicking with the left, reverse your stance, putting your left foot in back. Remember to stand erect, keeping your back straight at all times.

In this stance the power of your kick is increased. For extra strength ex-tend your hip as you extend your kick. As your balance improves, you can fin-ish your kick by setting the kicking foot down either in front or in back of the stable foot. For power, practice kicking a cushion or a bag.

Initially you will probably be more comfortable in bare feet. After you learn to kick without shoes, try kicking in all the different kinds of shoes you wear. You will find that your balance varies with each pair. You may expe-rience extreme difficulty balancing in certain shoes—I hope you throw away those shoes.

The ankle movement that gave you so much trouble in the beginning pro-tects your foot from injury and increases the power of the kick. You will find that the protective function of the ankle movement is less important when you are wearing sturdy footwear. The ankle motion is also not applied when your

target is the groin. In this case the best results come from bringing your foot up under the testicles and striking with the top part of your foot.

Another factor that influences a kick is your dress. In choosing your clothes, consider whether they give you enough freedom of movement to protect yourself.

It takes practice to develop the ability to judge the distance of your kick. Practice kicking an object, moving it to different spots to study your kicking distance. When your attacker is too far away for your kick, you will either have to wait for him to come into range or move toward him. When he is too close, you probably won't have as much control over the distance. Techniques that employ elbows and knees can be used in close situations more effectively than the longer-range punch and kick.

Elbow

The elbow, since it is sharp and hard, is a very effective weapon. When using elbow techniques, bend your elbow tightly and place your fist as close to your shoulder as you can. To avoid injury, lock your elbow, stabilizing the joint by tensing the muscles around it. Swing your elbow in a wide arc to maximize your power.

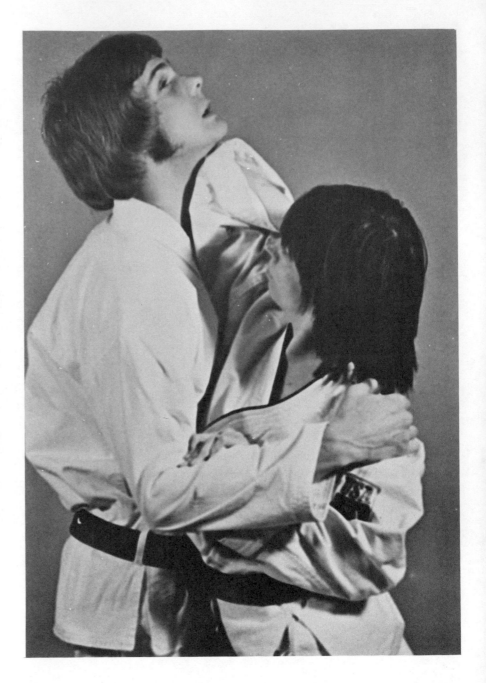

Upward Elbow Strike

To begin, assume the starting position for the punch. Point the elbow straight behind you; align your fist close to your body, forced toward your shoulder. Keeping your elbow in close to your body, swing it forward and straight up to the front. The best target for this strike is under the chin—or the nose, if you miss the chin. An upward elbow strike is generally too weak a blow to have any effect on the torso.

Downward Elbow Strike

Assume a fighting stance (see chart 3). Lift your elbow up as high as you can in front of you, keeping your fist close to your shoulder. Bring your elbow forcefully straight down, locking it into position about six inches in front of your solar plexus.

This technique is fairly specialized. It is useful for striking the base of the neck or the spine of someone who is bending over (after you have kicked him). Another possible target is the kidneys.

Front Elbow Strike

Force your elbow back toward your spine, with your fist just above your breast, palm down, and knuckles front. Grabbing the fist of the striking elbow with your other hand reinforces your power. Swing your elbow in a circular arc across your chest. Stop when your elbow points straight to the front. Your fist should be wedged firmly against your chest. Depending on the exact position of the attacker, this blow may be directed toward a jaw or a rib cage.

Side Elbow Strike

Stretch your right arm across your chest, right fist close to the left shoulder, palm down. Your left hand may grip your right fist. Move your elbow in a straight line across your chest. End with your elbow in a position directly to the side of your body, or pointing slightly behind. This blow may be directed to the stomach, solar plexus, groin, or face of an assailant.

Back Elbow Strike

Bring your fist to the front of your face, so that you are looking at the curl of your fingers. Point your elbow down. You may grip your fist with your other hand as in other strikes. Drive your elbow straight down and to the back. Your fist should stop close to your rib cage, and the elbow should point straight back. This blow will probably be directed to the solar plexus or the groin of an assailant holding you from behind.

Knee

A knee can be used in much the same way as an elbow, except that it has a much smaller range of motion. Consequently it generates less force. The only variation in kicking with your knee is in the target.

The most likely target for your knee is the groin. If you are able to execute the kick from a fighting stance (see chart 3), you will enhance the power of your kick. The stance enables you to swing your knee in a wide arc, bringing it up into the groin of an assailant. As with the elbow techniques, the knee should be tightly bent, with the foot close to the hip throughout the arc.

Practice this kick also from standing straight up with your feet about shoulder's width apart. This stance looks natural and won't warn an attacker that you intend to act. You will notice a difference in distance between the two stances as well. Fighting stance enables you to cover a greater distance; the natural stance is more appropriate when the assailant is very close to you.

In addition to the groin, the head and stomach are good targets for such a kick. In some cases you will be able to grab an attacker's head or body and pull it in to meet the swing of your knee.

Close-In Techniques

When your assailant is very close to you, it is difficult to put him in your control because you don't have enough room to generate much force. Most of the techniques for fighting at close range are designed to give you room enough to use more forceful ones. They are also useful in awkward positions such as when you are thrown to the ground or pressed against a wall. Since your main objective is to gain room to maneuver, you should not rely on their effects, but should forcefully continue your defense once you have gained the advantage.

The first task when confronted by any assault is to examine the circumstances. An assailant who has managed to come close to you will in most cases grab you and attempt to hold you in some manner. Inventory your weapons: Are your arms pinned? Can you move your legs? What is the attacker's position in relation to your position? What targets are within your reach?

These questions will help you choose the most effective defense technique in a situation. Practice this thought process quickly. Have a friend cooperate by putting you in various holds while you go through the mental exercise of choosing a proper technique. In most situations there are several possible choices. Be sure to explore each one.

Strike to Eyes

If your attacker is very close to you, and you have at least one hand free, poke your fingers into one or both of his eyes. This makes it difficult for him to see temporarily, but in all likelihood it will not cause blindness. If he is wearing glasses, move your fingers up under the glasses and into the eyes.

Pressure on Nose

If you wish to move your assailant's head and neck back in order to break a hold or get out from under him, place the outside edge of your palm under his nose and push upwards. This will not disable him, but he will be forced to move in the direction you press until he can escape the pressure or relieve it. Try this on yourself to find out how it feels.

Clapping Hands on Ears

If you have both your arms free with room to swing, and can easily reach an assailant's head, clap your hands forcefully against his ears. Use a wide backswing with your arms. This will create pressure in the inner ear, causing temporary pain and, possibly, the loss of equilibrium. You will cause the greatest amount of pain if both hands hit the ears simultaneously. Even one hand on one ear will cause considerable pain and confusion if enough force is used.

Fingers under Jaw

If an attacker is facing you at close range, and you have both your hands free, you can use them to force his body away from you in much the same way that pressure is applied against the nose. Place a forefinger or thumb under

each of his jaws where the bones make a right angle. (Feel your own jaw to find the right spot.) Jab sharply upward. Since you are exerting pressure against a part of the body that cannot resist, an attacker must move away in order to break the pressure. One hand pressed against the Adam's apple will have the same effect.

Blocks

Frequently the initial attack a man makes against a woman is an attempt to apply a hold of some sort. A man usually doesn't consider a woman dangerous enough to punch, but when he encounters resistance, he may resort to a more traditional fighting style. To be prepared for this, study the concept of blocking or deflecting blows. When you see a blow coming, you can choose among several responses: dodging it, avoiding it, or blocking it.

There are many ways to block, and the easiest blocks that can be used in most situations are discussed here.

Four variations on the basic block are required for a woman to be able to protect all of her body. The head area, the most vulnerable and open to attack, is protected by the upward block. Protect your torso with one of the two mid-section blocks. Learn the downward block to protect your abdomen and groin area.

The starting position for all four blocks is the same. Take the fighting stance position. Pay particular attention to the position of your left arm. If you are right-handed, the most favorable stance will be with your left foot and hand forward, so you can block with your left and punch with your right hand. Left-handed people find the opposite stance is best. Practice both, because you never know what you might need. (The following blocks are described for the left hand on-guard stance.)

Your left hand is in the "on-guard" position. The elbow, bent at 90 degrees, is held four or five inches directly in front of your rib cage. Your fist is at a shoulder-level with the palm facing the shoulder.

Upward Block

Pull your fist toward you, decreasing the angle of your elbow. Raise your elbow until your wrist is at eye level. Swing your elbow to the left and up, so it comes to your head level. The angle of your forearm to your upper arm is now about 130 degrees. Your fist turns so that the little finger side is pointing in front of you and slightly upward. Hold your wrist straight at all times.

The action of the upward block is that of your forearm catching a blow directed toward your head and deflecting it to the side. Ideally the blow slides down the angle of your forearm and off your elbow, where it is rendered harmless.

Midsection Outward Block

Move your elbow to the left, slightly outside your torso, keeping it at the same level. Rotate your forearm 180 degrees, until the palm of your fist is facing away from your body.

The action of the midsection outward block is to catch a blow directed toward your trunk and move it to the outside of the attacker's body. This usually opens up his stomach and groin to your counterattack.

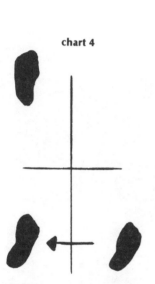

chart 4

Midsection Inward Block

Swing your elbow out to the left about six inches, then move it forcefully to the right. Keep your fist at the same level throughout the motion. At the same time move your right foot to the left and pull your hip back so your body is positioned in a sideways stance (see chart 4).

The action of the midsection inward block is to catch a blow directed toward your trunk and move it across the attacker's body. At the same time you pull your body out of the path of the blow. This usually opens up the assailant's ribs and kidneys to counterattack.

Downward Block

Move your fist in a downward arc to the right. Snap your fist down in front of your left leg, straightening your arm. Tense your elbow as your arm straightens out.

The action of the downward block is to catch a blow directed toward your abdomen or groin and move it away from your torso.

Blocking is a response to an action by someone else. Hence it takes timing and coordination. After you learn the basic motion of each block, practice your timing with a friend. Blocking is also a purely defensive motion. It won't save you from injury, and you must escape or move into a counterattack quickly. Practice combining each block you learn with a variety of counterattacks.

Multiple Attackers

When learning the basic techniques, it is easiest to assume a one-on-one situation. Unfortunately this is not always the case in actual assaults. A woman must be prepared for multiple attackers.

The techniques in this chapter will enable you to defend yourself against several attackers as long as none of them is able to hold you. Your position is strengthened if they do not work together smoothly or attack at once from more than one direction. It is important for you to have considerable freedom of movement, so you can maneuver yourself into the most favorable positions in relation to them.

Your strategy will be dictated in part by the situation. Some principles will help you construct your strategy.

1. Be acutely aware of the position of each attacker.

2. Pick out the one who is most unsure of himself. He will probably not initiate the attack and is more likely to leave himself vulnerable to a move from you.

3. Don't waste too much energy on the first attacker. Just stun him; take care of one or two more, and then return to the first just as he's recovering from the shock. The others will not be as stunned by your defense because the element of surprise will be lessened.

4. Be ruthless; try to disable attackers. You don't want to worry about one getting back up while you're busy with his buddies.

5. Know or discover the avenues of escape. Work toward them if you can. Spend as little time as possible fighting against bad odds.

In each succeeding chapter more principles for warding off multiple assailants will be added. As you progress and gain more skills, you will be able to handle many different types of situations.

PROBLEM 2:1—You are confronted by two assailants, coming toward you from opposite corners. The one on your left is closer to you than the one on the right. What can you do?

 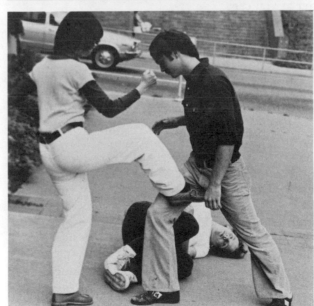

Program For Practice

The skills you learn from this book will help you only if you maintain them through a program of regular practice. The more you practice, the better your skills and reactions will become. Each person's lifestyle determines how much she will practice, but whatever you decide, make it regular and systematic. If you have friends who are also interested in learning self-defense, practicing together is helpful and fun. An arrangement to practice with a friend will also help you stick to your routine.

Consult an exercise book for warm-up exercises. You should never start practice cold. Do stretching and general conditioning exercises until you begin to sweat. Then you are ready to begin your practice without putting too much strain on your muscles and joints. Here are ways to practice each technique.

Punching

1. Punch ten times, alternating hands, slowly, from a natural stance. Concentrate on your form.

2. Punch ten times from the same stance, with as much speed and power as you can.

3. Punch slowly ten times in fighting stance, with each hand. Use right hand with left foot forward. Reverse your stance when you change hands.

4. Punch ten times each hand, fighting stance, for speed and power.

5. Punch ten times, each hand, striking a cushion. Fighting stance is best here.

Kicking

1. Kick ten times, alternating legs, as in Phase I, doing four steps separately. Don't stand against the wall unless you need its support.

2. Kick ten times slowly; then kick ten times for speed and power, as Phase I in one smooth motion. Alternate legs and stand away from the wall.

3. Kick slowly ten times with each foot from a fighting stance. Kick with the back foot. Then kick ten times each foot for speed and power. Reverse your stance when you change legs.

4. Kick ten times each foot kicking cushion or bag. Fighting stance is best here.

Blocking

Do each of the following exercises for the upward block, midsection outward block, midsection inward block, and downward block.

1. Block ten times slowly each hand, from fighting stance (use left hand with left foot forward); then block ten times with each hand for speed and power. Reverse your stance when you change hands.

2. Block ten times slowly with each hand, from fighting stance, combined with a counterpunch; then block ten times with each hand for speed and power.

3. Block ten times with each hand, and counterpunch with the other. Practice with a partner.

Elbow Striking

Do the following exercise for the upward elbow strike, downward elbow strike, front elbow strike, side elbow strike, and back elbow strike.

1. Practice each strike ten times slowly with each elbow, then practice ten times for speed and power.

Knee Kicking

1. Practice with each knee, ten times slowly and ten times for speed and power. First use a natural stance; then use a fighting stance, reversing the stance when you change legs.

Close-In Techniques

1. Have your partner grab you ten times. Each time decide quickly which technique could be applied in the situation and test it.

As you progress through the following chapters, increase your program of practice to include your new techniques and concepts. The counterattacks are the fundamentals of your self-defense program, however, and if you practice nothing else, practice these.

Chapter 3
Breaking Holds

The method that an attacker uses depends on what he wishes to accomplish. Usually a woman is confronted by an individual who wants something from her. This means the assailant has to get close enough to give directions—"Give me your money." "Take off your clothes." "Get into my car." And he will have to perform some action in relation to you that will frighten you enough to make you comply with his demands, but which will not disable you so much that you cannot do as he orders.

Putting you in a hold so that you have difficulty moving enables him to give you directions and convince you that you are in his power. There is something psychologically immobilizing about being held motionless against your will, even if you are not being hurt. A feeling of helplessness that leads to passivity is generated. If you can break the hold immediately and decisively, you will shatter the illusion of his power for both of you.

In many instances an assailant confronted with this rebuttal of his power gives up and tries to escape. Unfortunately this is not always the case, so you must be prepared to back up your break with the counterattacks described in chapter 2. Do not let the attacker reestablish his hold. Breaking it the second time will be much more difficult than was the first time. The second time he expects resistance, and you have lost the advantage of surprise.

Most people learning a martial art are especially eager to learn the techniques that will break a hold and enable one to throw an assailant across the room or land him on his head. To use these techniques successfully, you have to study a martial art diligently for a long time. They require skill, timing, and practice.

This chapter presents the easy techniques—the ones that simply break the hold. They are easy to learn and quick to apply, and can be used in various situations. A disadvantage of their use is that they leave you with a healthy attacker who could renew his attack. To offset this disadvantage, as you learn each break, practice combining it with various counterattacks.

If you see that someone is about to grab you, don't wait. The closer he is to you, the more his advantage in size and weight will serve him. If you start to fight before he gets his hands on you, you have a greater chance to control the action. Because a grab that comes from behind is more surprising and harder to handle, it is covered more thoroughly in this chapter. You should be able to anticipate and deflect those that come from the front. However, the same general principles apply regardless of the direction of the attack.

As a rule, men who attack women don't expect them to fight back; consequently, they are often not prepared for any resistance they meet. As a result, the strength applied to the hold is usually minimal and easily overcome. It may happen that you are grabbed in a very tight hold and don't have confidence that you can break it. This is the time to use pinching, biting, foot stomping, shin kicking, slapping, and other techniques that will not do any real damage other than to startle an assailant. As the attacker is startled, quickly take advantage of the temporary loosening of the hold to apply your break before he recovers. If you apply a startle technique to an area of his body away from the target spot of your main blow, you will pull his attention away from your real defense. Use such techniques routinely as insurance. Your *kiai* will have the same effect and will enhance the effect of whatever else you might be using.

If you feel you cannot break out of a hold, or if you try and fail, you need not give up the fight. In many cases you can afford to wait until you can take advantage of a better position. It is really hard for someone to rape you while he's holding you in a full nelson. Even a robber will have to let go in order to take your money. You can wait until he loosens the hold or releases you.

If you have to wait for your opportunity, catch the attacker when he is in motion. As long as his attention is divided between you and whatever he is doing, you have a better chance of taking him off guard. Even something as simple as talking divides his attention. If you decide to launch your defense while he is talking, hit him in the middle of a sentence. You can imagine how much being interrupted by a fist in the face disrupts concentration.

The longer you wait, the more you lose the psychological and strategic advantage. The longer you are in his power, the more opportunity he has to consolidate it. Waiting for the most opportune moment is a last resort tactic. An attacker is most unsure of himself at the beginning—your best defense will usually come at that time.

Wrist Holds

One very common method a man uses to attack a woman is to grab her wrist. If an assailant approaches from the front, there is no real need to break this hold, particularly if he has grabbed only one hand. You have the other

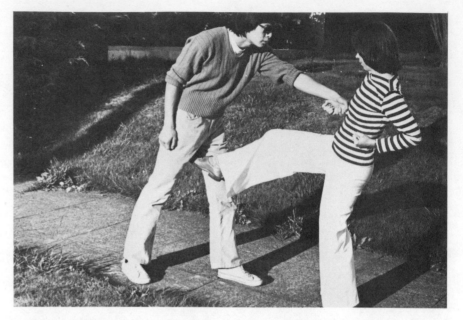

hand free to hit him, and both feet are free for kicking. You can even use his own attack against him by pulling him into your kick or punch.

But if you would rather get his hands off you altogether, there is an easy way to break this hold. The point where his thumb and fingers come together around your wrist is a weak point, and any pressure or motion involved in your defense should be directed toward this spot. First clench your fist; this will enlarge your wrist somewhat and weaken the hold from the outset. Then sharply twist your wrist in the same direction the attacker's thumb is pointing. If he is holding tightly, use your whole body in the twisting motion; turn your shoulders and hips at the same time. You may also grasp the held wrist with your free hand for extra power.

Drawing his arm straight out from his body also hampers his ability to resist. Speed and surprise are important elements of breaking this hold. Practice with a friend until you are able to respond very quickly.

As you practice you will discover that there are many variations of the wrist hold. The thumb and finger can end up in different sites on your wrist. Twisting toward the direction the thumb points is a good general rule. Some-

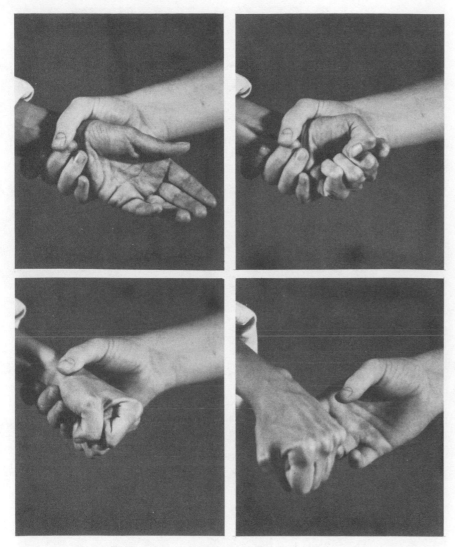

times, though, it will be more efficient to twist in the direction the fingers are pointing, still putting pressure on that weak juncture. Experiment with variations until you become comfortable with your response. When in doubt, though, always go in the direction the thumb points.

If he grabs both your hands from the front, break by twisting your wrists in opposite directions from each other. You may move them up and out or down and out.

If both your wrists are gripped from behind, bend your arms at the elbow and, twisting your wrists outward, pull your hands forcefully to the front. You may also combine the twisting motion of your wrists with a twist of your body, turning to face the assailant. This second option gives you more opportunity to continue your defense or to better evaluate your attacker.

If executed with speed and determination, these simple breaks will get you out of practically every conceivable wrist hold. You are then faced with the assailant and the possible need to continue your defense. You should now go on the offensive, trying to take control of the situation.

There are a couple of more complicated techniques that will put you in a more advantageous position to complete your defense. Both techniques involve breaking a hold on both your wrists. You must learn these techniques with a partner.

If held from the front, pull your hands in toward each other, as if to break the hold. As your partner tries to resist that motion by pulling outward on your hands, suddenly reverse your motion. Swing your and her hands quickly outward in a circle. If this does not break the hold, smash your partner's hands against each other at the top of the circle. Obviously, this must be toned down with a partner so you don't hurt her. Follow this with a quick counterattack, like a kick to the groin.

A wrist hold from the rear is sometimes difficult to break if your hands are held close together. A startle technique coupled with the simple break will usually do the trick, but here is another technique you can try.

chart 5

chart 6

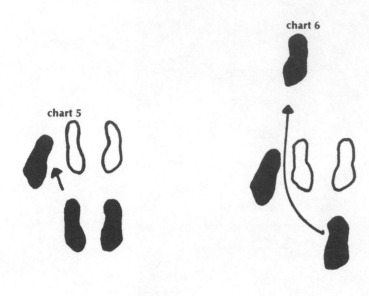

As your partner holds both your wrists behind you, first step back and out with your right foot at about a 45-degree angle. You will end up in a fighting stance, as shown in chart 5. As you move, swing your right hand up over your head, as your left hand moves down in opposition. You should be able to pass under your partner's right arm.

Pull her left arm, still holding yours, under her right arm. If she lets go of your wrist, grab hers. At the same time, step back with your left foot, leaving your right foot forward in a fighting stance, as shown in chart 6.

Pull down sharply on her right arm; this will force her to bend forward. At this point you can either let go of the left hand or continue to pin it under her right arm. As she bends forward, you will be able to use your kick as a counterattack, or you may choose to apply one of the arm locks from chapter 4. This maneuver will become easier for you after you have studied the arm locks. If you have difficulty now, return to this later.

PROBLEM 3:1 You are being held by a single attacker from the front; he is holding both your wrists. What can you do?

One-Arm Holds

There is a considerable number of variations in holds from the rear in-volving one arm of an assailant. He may hold you around the shoulders or the neck or clasp his hand over your mouth. He might use his other hand to rein-force the hold by grasping one of your arms.

The common feature of all the one-arm holds is that restraint is applied to the intended victim by partially encircling her with an arm. Such a hold has the same fundamental weakness as the wrist hold—it is weak at the point where the circle is not complete. The same kind of twisting motion can be ap-plied here as in breaking the wrist hold. Simply twist your shoulders sharply toward the gap; as you break the circle open, you can escape. If you secure his wrist as you escape the hold, you can apply an arm lock (see chapter 4).

  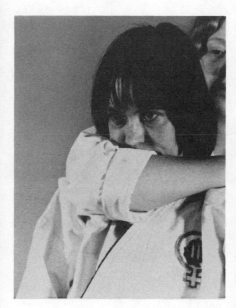 

If his grip is applied to your throat, you will not be able to twist away without putting pressure on your windpipe. To relieve the pressure, first use a back elbow strike with your free arm to loosen the hold, then quickly tuck in your chin to guard your throat. Next twist out in the basic break. Most of the following variations call for a sharp blow combined with the break. When you practice with a partner, be careful not to hurt her.

If the assailant holds your mouth and neglects to reinforce his hold by pulling your arm behind you, he affords you considerable freedom of motion. You can easily use a back elbow strike to his ribs or solar plexus, or one hand can reach his groin and strike or grab and twist the testicles. Any of these combined with the basic break should work quite nicely.

The elbow strike and hand to the groin can sometimes be used in other variations on this hold, depending on the position of his body relative to yours. Whenever someone is behind you, you must be careful to take into account the relative positions of your bodies. If you miss your target, you will tip him off to your intentions.

Defense becomes more difficult if an assailant reinforces his hold by gripping your arm (usually your left arm, if he is holding you with his right arm), but it takes him more time to apply this complicated hold. If you are alert, you can avoid the problem altogether by breaking out of his grasp before he has established it. Failing this, try to get out before he can twist your arm, which will make it painful for you to move.

If he is not twisting your arm, you should be able to free it with a little extra pull as you twist out of the hold. If his grip is especially firm, first try kicking his shin or stomping on his foot; then twist.

If he is twisting your arm, you will be hampered not only by the tightness of the hold, but also by the pain you will experience when you try to move. Ignore the pain as much as you can and devote your attention to escaping.

First move your body a little to the right (assuming his right arm is around your shoulders; reverse if he uses his left arm). Then quickly move back to the left to give yourself room for a right handed backward elbow strike to his ribs. Follow the elbow strike with a strike or grab to his groin. If he hasn't let go of you by this time, his grip should be loosened enough for you to twist away.

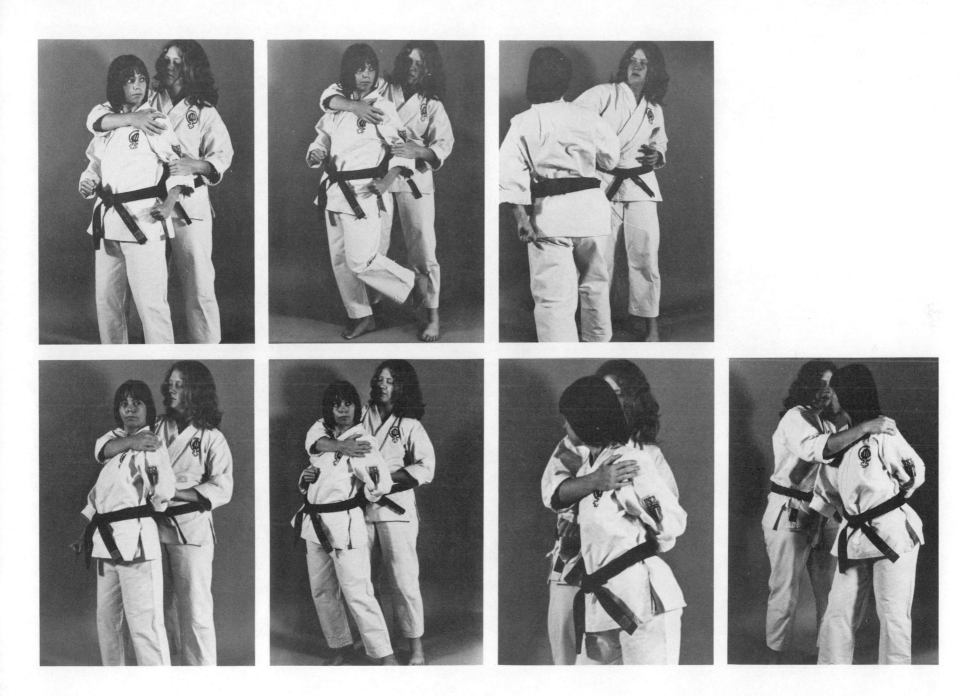

PROBLEM 3:2—You are being held by one assailant, one arm around your shoulders. What can you do?

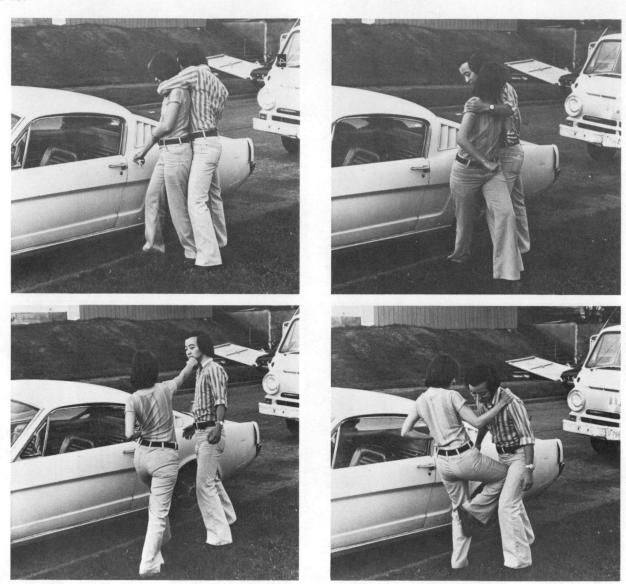

Bear Hugs

Bear hug attacks often seem indefensible since they envelope the intended victim so completely, pinning both arms. They actually are not very difficult to defend against because the attacker has taken quite a risk in getting in so close to you.

A potential assailant is in a particularly bad position when he tries a bear hug from the front. He will be pinning your upper arms to prevent you from reaching up, but you have almost total freedom of movement from the elbow down. Your target area will be restricted to below the waist, so don't be squeamish about attacking his groin.

Step back with one foot into fighting stance to give yourself more room. You will be able easily to reach his groin with your hands, or you can bring your knee right up into his groin.

In most situations you will be ready to defend long before he is close enough to grab you from the front. If he comes from behind, though, he may be able to surprise you. If you use a back elbow strike to the ribs in the bear hug, first sharply move your hips, taking your body out of the path of the strike and giving yourself a larger target area. A variation on this move is to strike the groin instead of sending your elbow into the assailant's ribs.

If you want to direct your efforts toward breaking the hold itself, follow these steps with a partner:

As your partner holds you in a rear bear hug, tuck your chin in to avoid choking and move your right foot out to the right, as shown in chart 7.

Keeping your back straight, drop your weight from your hips by bending your knees. Do not bend at the waist. Make sure that your feet are wide apart, giving you a wide base for your stance. If your feet are close together, you will probably fall over when you bend your knees.

Lace your fingers together and bring your elbows up and out to the sides to assist her arms in sliding off your shoulders.

After you have slipped out of the hold, you will be in a good position to deliver an elbow strike to the groin.

chart 7

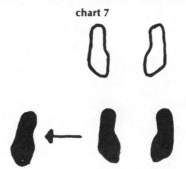

49

This break will not work if an assailant's arms are resting on your shoulders and around your neck instead of pinning your arms at your sides. In this case you are able to move your body more freely from side to side. Rely on your elbow to his stomach or ribs and your hand to his groin.

If he pins your arms below the elbows (unlikely unless he is short), a startle technique will help you break the hold.

Choke Holds

The important element in breaking a choke hold is to relieve the pressure on the throat as quickly as possible. If you fail to respond in time, you will pass out, and a state of unconsciousness is no position from which to defend yourself. There is also a danger of having your neck broken from a choke hold. As soon as you ensure that you will remain conscious, you can deal with the other features of the assault.

There are only a few variations on the choke holds. They are almost exclusively two-handed; it would take extraordinary size and power to strangle anyone with one hand. The possible variations are determined by the position of the assailant relative to the intended victim.

Front Choke Hold

Step back with your right foot into fighting stance. Clasp your hands together with your fingers laced. Your hands are hanging down, close to your left knee.

Keeping your hands together, raise them forcefully straight up over your head. First swing your hands up from the elbow until they are pointing upward. Then let your upper arms come into motion, finishing the swing from your shoulders. If you keep your elbows straight throughout the motion, you may hang your hands up in your partner's stomach and fail to break the hold.

As your arms sweep up between her two arms, the hold will be pulled off your throat with ease. You have your choice of counterattacks, with the most obvious being a kick to the stomach or groin with your right foot. Or you may simply bring your hands, still laced together, down onto the bridge of the nose.

Rear Choke Hold

If an assailant is trying to choke you from behind, you will not be able to use leverage in your favor as in the defense against the front choke. Grasp the little fingers of each of his hands and pull them sharply and forcefully out to the sides. Regardless of his strength, he will not be able to resist your motion.

Do not sacrifice speed and surprise for accuracy in this break. If you can't get the little fingers, any ones will do. The little finger is the weakest, with its neighbor being next in weakness. The strongest fingers are the first two, but even they are not strong enough to resist the pull of your hand. Take any finger—you don't even need a matching pair.

As you break the rear choke hold, put yourself in a favorable position for a counterattack. If you want to use punching or kicking or a combination,

quickly turn around and assume your fighting stance. You will have a good chance of applying an arm lock (see chapter 4) if you don't let go of his hand after you take it off your throat.

A choking attack from any other angle can be broken by one or the other of these techniques. Experiment with a friend to get an idea of the possibilities. When you practice breaking the rear choke hold with your friends, take care not to hurt them by jerking their fingers too sharply. In a life-threatening situation, of course, no such precautions are necessary.

Multiple Attackers

In multiple-attacker situations when a hold is applied by one attacker, the purpose is usually to hold the victim while some other assailant delivers the main blow of the attack. Such a hold usually comes from the rear, or some-

times from the sides, exposing the front of the intended victim to the attack.

The holds employed in such a situation are usually not dangerous in themselves. Their function is to make sure that the appropriate target remains available for the other attacker. Add the following principles to your collection on multiple attackers.

1. First determine who is going to deliver the main blow. In most situations you will have to deal with him first, before breaking the hold.

2. As you are held, make an inventory of the weapons you have available—feet, hands, knees, etc., and the techniques you can employ.

3. After warding off the main attacker, quickly break out of the hold and counterattack the holder.

4. If the attacker delivering the main blow is slow or far away, you may break the hold first. This is especially effective if you can time it so that the holder receives the blow meant for you, or if you are able to put the holder in the path of the attacker.

5. Use the holder's body as leverage in your defense against the main attack, if possible.

PROBLEM 3:3—An attacker is holding you in a rear bear hug. A second one is advancing toward you from the front. What can you do?

PROBLEM 3:4—Two attackers are each holding one of your wrists. They are standing out to either side of you. A third is advancing from the front toward you. What can you do?

Chapter 4
Take-downs

If your assailant does not run away as soon as you establish your defense, or if you wish to detain him, you will want to put him in a position from which he can do you no more harm. This is particularly crucial in situations in which you are alone or when you have to hold him until help comes. If you have knocked him out or otherwise disabled him, you won't have to worry about him for a while. But in any case, it is wise to establish and maintain your power to hold him.

Take-downs are methods of holding an attacker motionless as long as necessary. They require precise movement and are more difficult to execute than the counterattacks and breaking a hold. Most of these techniques require you to move in close, giving an assailant a chance to use his advantages in size, reach, and strength. Carefully evaluate each situation; use take-downs only when necessary or when little risk to yourself is involved.

Height is often an important factor in the effectiveness of take-down techniques. Make sure that you practice with people of various heights. With most of the take-downs, you can follow through with a counterattack to make sure that an attacker stays down without struggling. As you practice counterattacks

with the take-downs, take care that your posture is straight and firm. If you are off-balance, you may find yourself down on the floor with him.

If you ever have occasion to use one of these techniques, don't let false confidence lead you to dangerous inattention to the assailant. Do not relax your attention as long as your attacker is conscious.

Arm Locks

Several arm lock techniques are presented in this chapter, even though the same principles apply to each of them. If you understand the principles thoroughly, you can apply the appropriate arm lock in any circumstance.

The elbow and shoulder joints are the key points in arm locks. The elbow joint is a simple hinge joint. You are able to bend your arm at the elbow in only one direction—in toward your shoulder. From a straight-arm position your elbow does not bend back. The shoulder, on the other hand, has the greatest range of motion of any joint in the body. From the shoulder your arm can move in practically all directions.

In the arm locks the arm is used as a lever to control the rest of an opponent's body. The elbow joint must be locked to keep the arm straight; otherwise it loses the capacity to function as a lever. Pressure is then put on a shoulder joint in various ways to control and move the rest of the body. Arm locks work effectively regardless of the position of an attacker's feet. He is most vulnerable standing with his feet about a shoulder's width apart and least vulnerable when one foot is in front of the other.

Each locking technique is presented separately, so you can learn the basic moves. Study the problems to learn how to maneuver an assailant into the correct position. Practice these with a partner.

Arm Lock Number 1

Stand in fighting stance slightly behind and to the right of your partner. Grasp her right wrist with your right hand. Turn it inward until the palm is up. Pull your partner's arm to an outstretched position. This position locks the elbow; take care that you maintain it so that the arm does not bend.

Apply pressure with your left hand (gently at first, with a partner) at any spot between the elbow and the shoulder. This pressure will cause your partner to bend forward. Experiment with different positions for this pressure to find the best spot for you. Most people use either a position close to the elbow or one close to the shoulder. An inward rotary motion with your left hand applied just above the elbow and in the direction away from your partner's body is effective in forcing her body forward.

For pressure near the shoulder, the best motion is to come up under the back part of your assailant's joint with the heel of your palm or the outside edge of your hand. Then push up, in, and down in a rotary motion. If you raise your own arm to your side at shoulder height, you will be able to feel a triangular muscle running in the back under your arm, like a web from your shoulder blade to your upper arm. That is the spot you want to hit.

While your partner is bent over, you can use a front kick to the face or stomach. If you want to put her on the floor, just walk forward quickly a few steps, pulling her weight out in front of her feet. If this maneuver is executed with speed and strength, an attacker will quickly collapse to the floor with very little effort on your part. Practice slowly at first, until you understand exactly how the technique works for you. Then speed up, taking care not to hurt your partner as you practice.

PROBLEM 4: 1—One attacker is coming in from the front as he aims a punch at your face. What can you do?

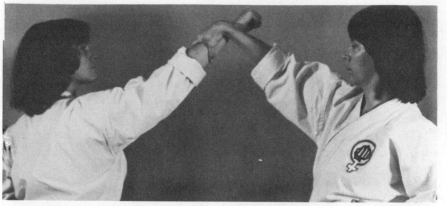

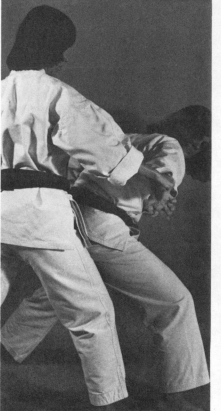

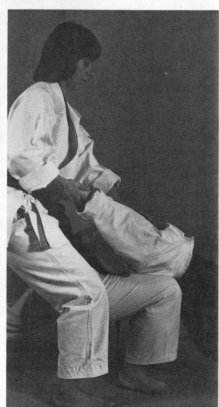

Arm Lock Number 2

This lock is actually just a variation on Number 1. It gives you a little more freedom to place your body in relation to an attacker, but its effectiveness is cut drastically if the assailant is considerably taller than you.

You may stand to the right of your partner anywhere in the space between your position for arm lock Number 1 to a right angle to her. The closer your position is to a right angle, the better the technique will work. You can keep more distance between you for this technique than for Number 1, since your hand does not need to reach shoulder level. Fighting stance is best but not necessary in this maneuver.

Grasp your partner's right wrist with both your hands. Pull your partner's arm to an outstretched position, turning her wrist clockwise until the palm faces up. Quickly turn the wrist toward the front of your partner's body. Pull her hand up so that it is higher than her shoulder, keeping her arm extended. Grip her wrist with your thumbs on the back of her wrist and your fingers curled around the inside of her palm. Bend her hand up to take slack out of her wrist.

Sharply push on the lever of the arm, driving the bone of the upper arm straight into the socket of the shoulder joint. Be careful to keep the hand higher than the shoulder. At the same time move forward to take your partner off balance.

As with arm lock Number 1, this technique can be used to hold an assailant in a bent-over position, unable to move and vulnerable to your kicks. Or use the technique to throw an attacker to the ground.

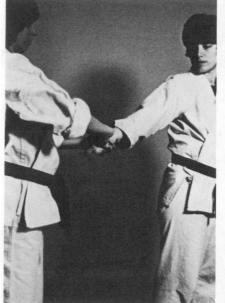
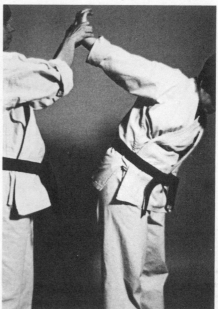

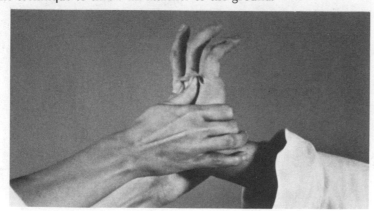

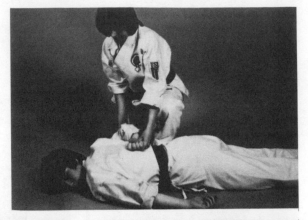

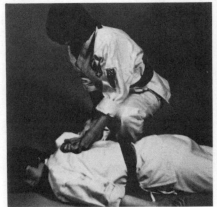

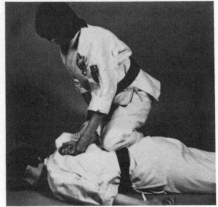

Once an assailant is on the ground, you can keep him there. He will usually fall face down (prone). Maintain your grasp on your attacker's (partner's) wrist. Pull her hand up behind her back, bending her elbow and keeping her wrist close to the back. Pull the hand toward the neck until both the shoulder and elbow joints are tight. Hold the elbow in with your right hand and elevate it. Kneel down behind the elevated elbow, placing your left knee directly below the shoulder blade and put your weight on it. From this position an attacker will have trouble moving at all, much less getting up.

PROBLEM 4:2—A single attacker is coming in from the front aiming a punch to your stomach. What can you do?

Arm Lock Number 3

An arm lock applied from in front of your attacker leaves you vulnerable to further attack from him. When you are off to the side or behind him, an attacker can't reach you easily, but if you use an arm lock from the front, you must follow it with a counterattack, or else quickly move to a position of greater safety.

Standing in front of your partner, assume a fighting stance. Grasp her right wrist in your right hand; pull it towards you to extend her arm. Keep her palm facing up and her wrist pulled back to lock the elbow. Your left hand forms a fist; swing it up under your partner's upper arm above the elbow, hitting (gently, with your partner) with the part of your fist that forms a ring with the thumb and forefinger. Hold your partner's wrist firmly, so your blow strikes a rigid arm that cannot give way.

If you strike with considerable force, you may break your attacker's arm or sprain his elbow. Less force will drive the head of the attacker's upper arm bone up across the socket of his shoulder joint. The shoulder joint socket is shallow, and the sudden movement causes considerable pain and forces an assailant off balance in an attempt to relieve the pain.

Practicing with your partner, hold your fist against her arm, applying steady pressure to hold her off balance.

From this position you can use a kicking counterattack. You can pull her suddenly forward and let her fall, or you can move your body around to the side, apply an inward rotary motion with your left hand, and change into arm lock Number 1.

PROBLEM 4:3—A single attacker moves in from the front with a punch to your midsection. What can you do?

chart 7

chart 8

Arm Lock Number 4

This technique is a variation on arm lock Number 3. It uses the same principle of downward force on the forearm, coupled with upward force on the upper arm. As you face your partner, grasp her right wrist in your left hand. Pull her arm forward to extend it. Move your right foot in front of you and a little across the midline of your body; then pivot on both feet so you end up facing the opposite direction in a fighting stance with your left foot forward as shown in charts 8 and 9. At the same time pull your head under your partner's arm and bring her arm down across your left shoulder. Rotate her hand outward until its palm faces up. (For a short attacker, turn the opposite direction and pull his arm down across your shoulder without going under his arm.) Extend her arm fully so the elbow is forced into a locked position. Your shoulder is applying the upward pressure on the upper arm. Pull down sharply on her wrist to exert a downward force on the forearm.

Be sure to position your body so an assailant cannot reach you with his other hand. The best counterattack from this position is a strike to the groin or an elbow to the ribs or solar plexus.

Arm locks Numbers 3 and 4 must be varied to compensate for differences in height between the two participants. Experiment with partners of various heights. Generally the place where force is applied to the upper arm should be lowered in proportion to how much taller an attacker is in relation to his intended victim. If he is shorter than you, you will have the advantage.

PROBLEM 4:4—A single attacker is coming in from the front and aiming a punch at your face. What can you do?

Tripping Techniques

While the arm locks work effectively regardless of the position of the attacker's feet, the tripping techniques work best on someone who is standing with one foot forward. While learning the basic technique, keep your right foot forward in all cases. After you master each technique, try it with your other foot forward. (In fact, you should practice all techniques on both sides.)

Tripping techniques are used in response to an assailant's movements. If someone is standing and merely threatening you, you can't walk up and trip him. It is when he is in motion, moving toward you, reaching for you, that his balance is off and you can bring him down easily. Tripping is basically a redirection of the attacker's momentum. As he moves forward, place your foot behind his front foot to prevent him from adjusting his balance on his next

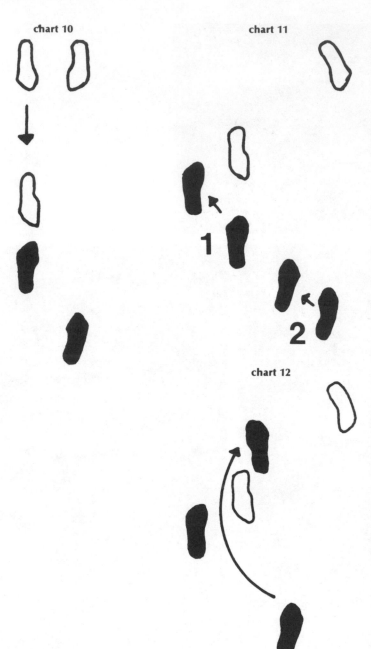

chart 10

chart 11

1

2

chart 12

66

step. At the same time apply force backward to a vulnerable or weak area on his body. Unable to adjust his balance because of your foot behind his, he will fall backward. There are two basic variations on tripping, depending on the direction of the attack. The footwork is the most important element in tripping. Practice these techniques with a partner.

Direct Attack

Your partner steps forward on her right foot, reaching straight in toward you with her right hand as an attacker would. As she moves in, move your left foot out diagonally from your left side. Position yourself in fighting stance, as shown in charts 10 and 11. In this position your body is also out of the path of the blow.

You may want to use your left hand in an inward blocking position (see chapter 2) to make sure that your partner's right hand is incapable of counterattack. You won't have to worry about her left hand because she won't be able to reach you with it. Move your right foot around to a position just behind your partner's right foot, as shown in chart 12. Keep your right leg straight so that she can easily fall over it.

Your right hand applies the backward force. Its movement is determined by the position of your partner's right hand and arm in relation to you. In a real attack you can move your arm over an attacker's arm to hit or push his throat to move him backward. From the same position move your right arm under an attacker's right arm and bring your hand up to put pressure on his right shoulder. To practice with a partner, start with the heel of your palm under her arm, close to the armpit, and use a circular motion to first press up from underneath and then push down. You can also direct your pressure to the throat from the underarm position.

Circular Attack

If an attacker approaches you with a circular motion of his arm, you will not be able to move outside the arm's path, but will have to go to the inside. Moving in on an attack is not a natural reaction and takes determination and practice. You must move in very close to the attack. Consequently you have to move quickly, before an attacker has a chance to react.

As your partner moves in, use an outward block with your left hand (assuming she is attacking with her right) as you move in closer to her body. If you move away, your block will not be as effective, and you will not end up in a position to take her down. (This doesn't mean you should never move away. Sometimes you may want to sacrifice your chance for a take-down for some other advantage.)

As you move in, assume fighting stance, left foot forward, as you block, as shown in chart 13. Since you can't move outside her reach, turn your body with your block so that your right shoulder is approximately facing her. Keep your blocking arm in position; you can grab your partner's attacking arm with your left hand. Then move your right foot around behind her right foot, as shown in chart 14. Your right hand moves either to her throat or to her shoulder. As you push her back and down, twist your hips into the pushing motion to give yourself extra strength and more leverage for your tripping leg.

In all variations of the tripping techniques, your movements must be quick and decisive. When you are practicing with a partner, however, don't release your hold on her as she goes down. This will protect her from hurting herself as she falls. In a real situation, of course, how an assailant lands is his problem.

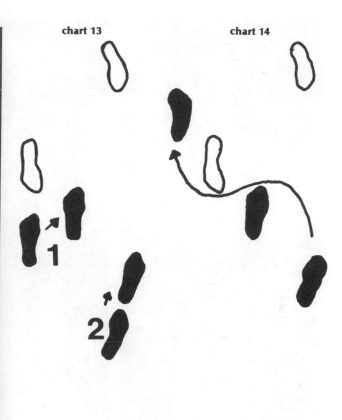

 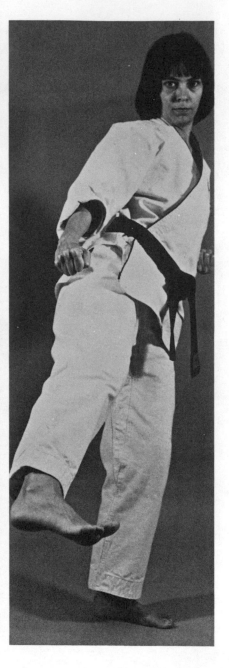

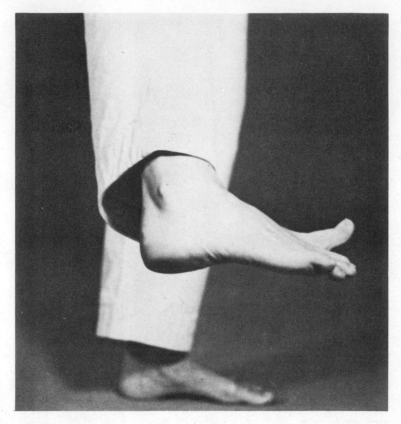

Knee Kick

A kick to the knee can be used as an offensive technique in itself or as an aid to a take-down. The basic motion is the same in either case. First lift your knee straight in front of you as high as you can. This first step is similar to the first step in the front kick.

Thrust downward at a 45-degree angle to the side (left side for left foot). Point your toes toward the center of your body at the same angle as your hip, which will turn into the kick. Strike with the edge of your heel.

For balance, let your arm swing in the same line as your leg on the same side. Keep your opposite hand clenched in a fist at your side, ready to punch after the kick. After the kick is extended, pull your foot back to its original position, and then set it down again.

This type of kick is slower than a direct kick to the knee. It has the advantage of generating great power through its long downward thrust. The higher you bring your knee in the first step, the more power you will be able to deliver to the target. You will have more success using this kick in combination with other techniques, especially ones that move you out to the side of the attack. A disadvantage, in addition to slowness, is that this kick requires a lot of room. When you are held close to an assailant, a sharp swing from your knee is the best kick to use.

It is not important with the knee kick that the assailant be in motion, but forward movement on his part does enhance the effectiveness of the technique. It is also helpful, though not necessary, that the attacker have one foot placed in front of the other. (Once again, assume for purposes of practice that his right foot is forward.)

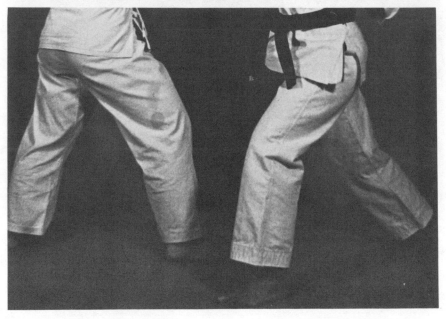

chart 15

As your partner moves in, step out with your left foot at a 45-degree angle, as in the tripping movement. (See chart 15.) You can block, if necessary, but the block will be auxiliary since you will have moved your body from the path of the blow. Grasp your partner's right arm, shoulder, hair, sleeve—anything you can reach on the upper part of the body.

As you execute the kick, direct it to the back part of the front knee. Sharply pull your partner's upper torso in the opposite direction of the kick. This will force her to land directly in front of you in easy reach of your counterattack. With your partner, the back part of the knee is the safest target; with an actual attacker, the side of the knee is more vulnerable to injury.

If an assailant is attacking with a circular motion, you will not be able to use the knee kick if you have to move inside his attack. It is usually better in such cases to use a tripping technique.

Stomp Kick

The knee kick is effective as a counterattack on someone who has fallen down. To modify the knee kick into a stomp, first raise your knee directly in front of you. Then thrust downward to the front, leading with the heel. The striking surface is the heel proper in this variation, rather than the side of the heel. Before using this kick, you will have to evaluate whether a counterattack is necessary and to what extent it should be employed. The kick can be delivered to stomach, chest, groin, or head, depending on how much damage you want to do. The resistance of the floor or ground removes the ability of the attacker's body to give with the blow and increases the effect of your kick.

Standing over a person lying at your feet can be an awkward position in which to deliver an effective blow, and it is important that you not lose your

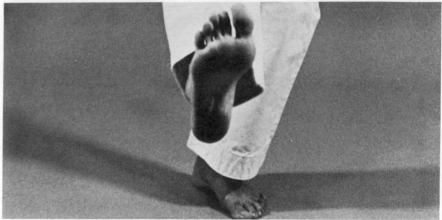

balance while delivering a counterattack. Whether you are using a punch or a kick, always keep your upper body erect, lowering yourself by bending your knees. The stomp kick directed straight downward has the advantage that you don't have to worry about lowering your body. You can remain completely erect. Remember, of course, to pull your foot back quickly, so an attacker can't grab it and use it to bring you down.

PROBLEM 4:5—The attacker is coming in from a 45-degree angle in front of you and to your left. He steps in with his left foot, reaching for you with his right hand. What can you do?

Multiple Attackers

Since take-downs are relatively slow techniques, they are difficult to use in multiple-assailant attacks. With more than one assailant, you need to dispatch each one quickly and turn to deal with the next one. Here are some suggestions:

1. If one attacker is close to you and the other(s) are too far away to get to you quickly, you can use a take-down on the one that is close. If possible, make him land in the path of one of the others so the second one has difficulty reaching you. It should be disturbing to the other(s) to see their buddy on the ground, and they might just give up and leave.

2. If you have already dealt sufficiently and quickly with the first attacker(s), you will have plenty of time to use a take-down with the last one, just as if he were a single assailant.

3. In some situations, you may be able to use an arm lock on one attacker while directing a kick to another.

PROBLEM 4:6—There are two attackers, in opposite 45-degree corners in front of you. The one on the left is close; the one on the right is farther away. The assailant on the left punches with his right hand. What can you do?

PROBLEM 4:7—There are three attackers: two at opposite angles 45 degrees in front, and one directly in front of you. The one on the left grabs your shoulder; the one in front advances. What can you do?

Chapter 5
Weapons Defense

A weapon in the hand of an assailant increases his physical and psychological power. And it increases your risk of injury. Any assault involves risk of injury. Often the risk has little or nothing to do with whether or not you choose to fight back. The psychological power of a weapon is so great that many of us immediately opt for submission in the hopes of avoiding serious injury. And fighting back does hold more potential for injury when a weapon is involved. Yet submission carries with it a corollary risk. Surrender does not guarantee that an attacker will not use a weapon. Remember, criminals don't play fair. A weapon situation, therefore, demands careful consideration.

The use of a weapon by men who attack women is similar to the use of the hold. The purpose of the weapon is usually that of a threat. An assailant displays a weapon clearly to an intended victim in order to frighten her into submission. Sometimes he doesn't intend to use the weapon at all; sometimes he'll use it only if he feels it is necessary. And sometimes he intends to use the weapon *regardless of your reaction*. In most cases when he intends to use the weapon, it will be after he has obtained what he wants. Your surrender is part of his plan; it doesn't, in such a case, reduce the violence of the assault.

The problem of psychologically evaluating an assailant carries extreme importance in such situations. You have to figure out whether an attacker is likely to use the weapon. You also have to weigh the risk you take in fighting back against what you stand to lose by surrendering.

A weapon produced in the course of a struggle is more likely to result in injury than one displayed at the beginning of the assault. The same is true of impromptu weapons picked up in the surrounding area during the struggle. In the midst of a fight, threat is almost useless. The only value gained from a weapon at this point is a greater capacity for causing injury. In such a case, you may have no alternative but to fight back. It is best to be ready psychologically, just in case defense against a weapon becomes a physical necessity.

The most difficult situation in which to deal with a weapon is the one in which the primary aim of the attacker is to injure or kill you. If you don't have a warning and time to respond, your chance of escaping without injury is relatively small. In most assaults on women, though, the weapon is intended as a threat — a means of coercing the woman to comply with the attacker's demands. Each technique discussed in this section assumes that the principal purpose of the weapon is intimidation. The same techniques, however, can be applied in other circumstances.

If you are ever confronted by a weapon, you will have to carefully evaluate both the attacker and the circumstances of the attack. Most weapons are extensions of the arm of the one who wields them. If you choose to fight back, or are forced to, most of the same principles and techniques presented in earlier chapters will apply.

A gun, in contrast to other weapons, has greater power, since it is not confined to a role as an extension of the arm. Its ability to cause injury from a distance makes defense against it a delicate proposition. So many variables are available with a gun that the scope of this book cannot embrace adequate treatment of all possible defenses. Unfortunately, the power of the gun that makes defense so risky also makes surrender more risky. Much will depend on the circumstances and the individuals involved.

Knife

While a knife adds to the assailant's power, it lacks many of the advantages of a gun. Whereas a gun can inflict injury from a distance, a person with a knife must come as close to his intended victim as an unarmed assailant. He must expose himself to the danger of a counterattack. A knife is slower than a gun and carries less capacity for accuracy and disabling injury.

Nevertheless, most people are intimidated into immediate submission at the sight of a knife in an assailant's hand. We have a natural aversion to spilling our own blood that hinders us in resistance. As long as the knife is there, there is a risk of your being cut; however, it is often worth the risk of minor cuts on your arms and legs to avoid major cuts in vital areas. Your attitude toward a knife attack should be to protect yourself from serious injury, not simply to avoid bloodshed.

Each situation is different; you will have to weigh your attacker's advantage, your risk, his psychological state, and whatever you have at stake. If you do choose to fight back, there are a few principles that apply to practically all the techniques presented below.

1. Protect yourself from direct cuts. If you have a jacket or a sweater, wrap it around your arm to minimize cuts. A pillow or purse can be used to trap the knife like a skewer. Side-stepping movements remove your body from the direct path of the knife.

2. Direct your defense against the hand holding the knife rather than against the knife itself.

3. Once the assailant is disarmed, try to make the knife inaccessible to him. Kick or throw it out of the way. Do not attempt to use it on him unless you are very sure of yourself—both in terms of how much injury you need to cause him and of your own expertise. You don't want to put yourself in a position from which an angered attacker can take a knife back from you.

In practicing the following techniques with a friend, do not use a sharp knife. Even with a substitute you can still tell whether or not you *would* have been cut, and there aren't any accidents with a substitute.

Thrusting Attack from the Front

As your partner extends her arm with a knife, move forward and to the side with your left foot in the same pattern described in chart 11. With your left foot forward, use an inward block with your left hand to block the arm or hand that is holding the knife. Your body should be well out of the path of the knife as a result of the side-stepping. The purpose of the block is to control the knife more than it is to change its direction. If possible, use padding of some sort to protect your own hand and arm from cuts.

While an assailant is still dazed by the failure of his attack, you can deliver a counterattack such as a kick or punch. You can also apply an arm lock or use the knee kick as a take-down. If you use enough force in the block, or in the

follow-up techniques, an attacker will probably lose the knife. Be sure to secure the knife as soon as you can afford to let go of him.

Descending Attack from the Front

Use the same footwork against a stab coming from above as against a thrusting front attack. It is easier for an assailant to generate more force with a downward motion of the knife, so you will have to take particular care to get your body out of the way, and you'll have to use considerable power in your block.

When practicing, have your partner move the knife downward as you apply an upward block. Follow with a counterattack, arm lock, or a take-down.

Slashing Attacks

If an attacker swings a knife in a wide arc in front of him, hoping to catch you with it at some point in the arc, you will have a hard time blocking the knife or disarming him. He is committing himself to a motion that takes longer than a direct attack, however, and he will have difficulty altering his course. Your best defense is to deprive him of a steady target. Move around a lot, dodge the path of the knife, back away.

If you have a jacket, coat, curtain, towel, or something similar, use it to trap the knife. Attempting to trap a knife with a smaller object is more difficult because of the wide arc of its path. Something large enough to cover the arc will trap the knife successfully. Trapping it also has the advantage of allowing

you to stay at a greater distance from an assailant, an action that reduces your danger. Experiment with your partner to get a feel for the necessary timing and distance involved in this strategy (see page 96 for further discussion).

In a slashing attack there are two points in the swing where an assailant is weakest. One is at the beginning of the backswing, as his arm is forced back toward his body. The other is in the follow-through, as his arm crosses his body. Your movement must be timed carefully, to take advantage of this weakness. Padding is especially important if it is available. If you move in on the backswing, make sure that you disarm the attacker; if he manages to free his arm, he will be able to stab you. On the other hand, if you move in on the follow-through, it is easier to trap the knife in a safe position. This is the strategy I recommend.

In practice, as your partner swings a knife in front of her, step in close as soon as the knife passes the front of her body and travels to the opposite side. Once you are in close enough to disrupt the return of the arm, use an outward block with your right hand to trap it. For a counterattack use a left elbow to the chin or a knee into the groin. You won't be in a very good position for an arm lock, but some of the tripping techniques will work as a take-down.

Attacks From The Rear

In order to defend yourself against a knife, you have to be able to see where it is aimed. In an attack with a knife from the rear, you first will have to perceive the threat, then turn and meet the attack. After you turn, use the same techniques as you would if the attacks came from the front.

If an assailant is merely attempting to frighten you by producing a knife, and wishes to stay behind you, he will still have to let you know the knife is there. He will have to come close to you without alarming you, and will probably carefully touch the knife to some part of your body. At the same time he will be giving you directions or admonishing you not to scream. I hope that you are sufficiently vigilant in your own defense that no one will be able to put you in this position. Once you are in it, it is difficult to get out.

Speed and force are very important in these situations, because a knife that is already touching you doesn't take much time to cut. Still, it's not impossible to defend yourself, although you may opt to wait for a more opportune moment. Since an attacker from behind can't do very much either, you may be able to afford to wait.

Knife at Throat

One of the most horrifying prospects of being attacked by a knife-wielding assailant is having him manage to get a hold on you from behind and put a knife to your throat. This attack is one that requires considerable time on an assailant's part, so only in the most extreme circumstances should you have failed to begin your defense by the time he has you in his grip. If he has managed to grasp you, though, your first strategy should be to try to wait until he is in a more vulnerable position.

Practice resisting such an attack. As your partner holds you, work one of your hands up, ready to come between your throat and the knife (substitute) or her hand that is holding the knife. Then tuck your chin in and apply the same break that you would use against a one-arm grab (see chapter 3).

This is obviously a last-ditch defense technique. There is considerable risk involved; the closer the knife is to your throat, the greater the risk.

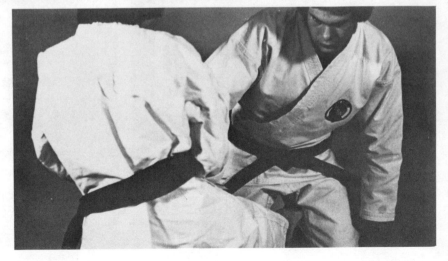

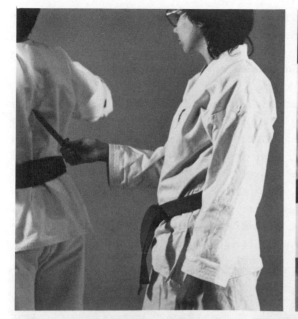

Knife Point In The Back

A common scare tactic among men who assault women is to come from behind, put the tip of a knife in your back, and give directions from that position. A good percentage of the time, it's not really a knife, but just his finger. Depending on how you are dressed, you may be able to figure out which it is, if you have practiced distinguishing between knives and fingers in the comfort of your own home.

If an attacker doesn't grab your arm from the rear as well, the defense against this attack is not difficult. As your partner holds a knife substitute in your back, raise your right arm, extending it to the side. Sharply and suddenly turn your body toward your right. At the same time swing your right arm out and back to knock the knife substitute out of her hand. As your body turns, the target moves out of the path of the knife. Your right arm then deprives the attacker of his weapon. You still end up very close to him, but you have a variety of follow-up techniques at your disposal.

If he reinforces his attack by grabbing your arm, he will probably hold your left arm with his left hand, leaving the knife in his right hand. In this situation turning to the left instead of the right will make it easier for you to get your body out of the way, but it will be more difficult to disarm him since you will not have freedom to swing your arm in a very wide arc. If his grip is very strong, it is probably better to go to the left; if it is weak, ignore it and go to the right.

Club

A club is a difficult weapon to conceal or carry around. Most often it is an impromptu weapon snatched up in the heat of battle. Your chances, then, of being confronted with a club are much less than those of facing a knife. A club does present some unique problems, worthy of discussion here.

Envision a club as a heavy, long extension of an assailant's arm. It is ex-

tremely difficult in the middle of a fight to gauge accurately how much length is added to an attacker's reach by a club. Consequently, a swinging club is often harder to dodge than a swinging knife. The length of a club also provides a greater margin of error for dodging, especially since the club can inflict injury at any point along its length.

The weight of a club adds to its potential for injury, but also makes it a difficult weapon to wield. This is especially true where the speed of an attack is concerned. Speed is greatly hampered by the weight and bulkiness of a club. Dodging may be made more difficult by the uncertainty of the length of the club, but the lack of speed is an advantage in that you have extra time to move. If you have enough room to move, dodging may be a good ploy. You will be able to exaggerate distances to provide for the extra length of the club. If you are in a small space, you will probably have to combine your dodge with a counterattack designed to end the assault.

Clubs are efficiently used in wide, swinging motions. The two common swings are an overhead downward swing and a sideways swing across the body. An attacker is most vulnerable at the beginning and end of his swing. Your goal is to avoid contact with the club and try to deal with the arm holding it instead.

Make a practice club out of rolled-up newspaper for yourself. Try swinging it to get the feel of what you could be up against. You won't experience exactly the same thing as with a real club since a paper club is very light, but the essential principles should be clear. You will notice that you need plenty of time for your swing, and that the greatest amount of power is generated at the end of the club, where the arc is widest. If you try to hit something that is so close to you that your arm has to bend quite a bit, you will have considerable difficulty building up power and hitting your target. This is why some of the techniques that follow are based on the tactic of moving in close to a club

wielder. The idea of moving into an attack may seem frightening, but it is an efficient and effective way to deal with a club assault. When you move close, your purpose is to restrict an attacker's arm and club by taking away the necessary distance.

Immobilize the Backswing

As your partner draws her arm back in preparation to swing a club, step in with your left foot close to her body, inside the range of her extended arm. You will end with your left foot forward in fighting stance.

With your left hand use an outward block to catch her arm in the backswing. The farther back in the swing that her arm is trapped, the harder it will be to resist. Your right hand is free for a counterattack that almost certainly will be necessary. For a counterattack use an elbow strike to the chin or any

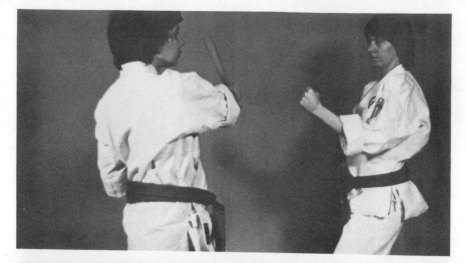

type of knee or hand blow to the groin. In most situations a take-down is easy after the counterattack.

Experiment trapping the arm of your partner. Let her swing her arm back. Catch her arm at various angles and try to hold it back while she tries to bring it forward. From this you can experience the variations in strength according to the angle at which you catch the arm.

Trap the Follow-Through

As with the knife slasher, the club wielder is vulnerable just as his arm completes the arc and passes to the other side of his body. The weight of the club makes it even more difficult for him to bring his arm back in opposition to your force. As your partner swings her club, step into fighting stance with your left foot forward. Trap her arm with an inward block of your left hand.

For a counterattack, elbow and knee techniques are best since you are in so close.

Descending Club Attack

For an overhead club swing coming downward at you, use the same defense technique you would use against a similarly moving knife. (See page 80.) Use your side-stepping footwork to go outside the club's path, and then move in close to your partner. Apply the upward block to the arm holding the club. Take particular care to block with force, and quickly follow through with a counterattack. From outside the path of the club, grab your partner's hair or collar with your left hand and pull sharply downward. At the same time bring your right foot up and deliver a knee kick to her right knee. It should bring her down. Remember to hit the *back* of her knee to avoid injury.

In all the techniques be sure to move in close enough to the assailant to reduce the effectiveness of the club. As you practice with your partner, using a rolled-up newspaper for a club, let her penetrate your block to hit you. In this way you can study the difficulties of the club wielder in trying to hit a close target. You will be able to see how close you need to move in to be safe.

Multiple Attackers

If one or more of the group of attackers displays a weapon, you must give him the highest priority.

1. Do not expose yourself to attack by a weapon while you are giving your attention to one of the other assailants.

2. If a weapon wielder is farther away from you than an unarmed attacker, you may be able to confront the unarmed one while blocking the path of the attack of the armed one.

3. You may use the unarmed assailants to cover your escape if the path of escape is far enough from the weapon holder.

4. One or more unarmed assailants may try to hold you while another one advances with a weapon. It is usually best to deal first with the weapon. If the weapon attack is slow, however, you may be able to pull one of the holding attackers into its path.

PROBLEM 5:1—There are two attackers, one with a club. The unarmed one is close to you; the other is distant. What can you do?

PROBLEM 5:2—There are three attackers. Two are holding you, one on either side. The third advances in front of you with a knife. What can you do?

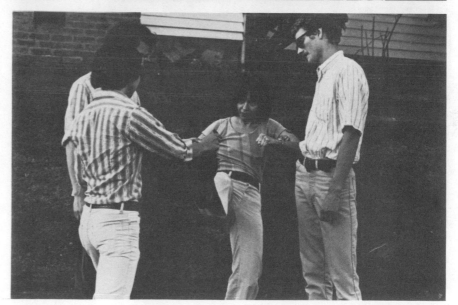

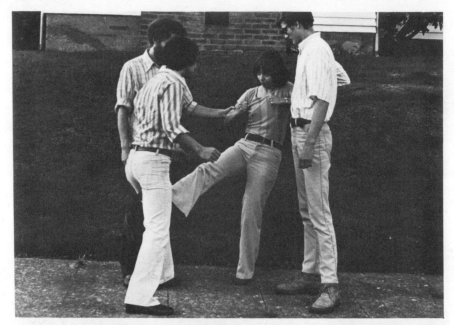

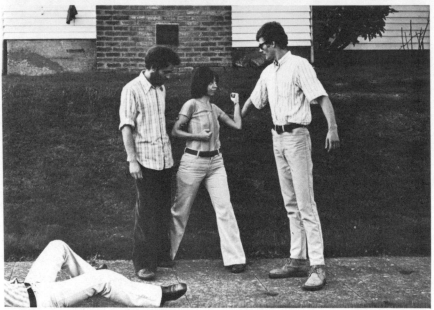

Chapter 6
Impromptu Weapons

A fellow karate instructor once told me that when a woman interested in self-defense comes to him, he tells her, "Buy a gun." The question of a woman's use of weapons comes up repeatedly in discussions about self-defense. This instructor represents one prevalent view on the subject. He belongs to the group that believes that a woman must rely on technology to make her equal in power to her assailants. Others believe that a woman is not strong enough to control technology and should stay away from weapons because an assailant could take the weapons away and use them against a weak, inept woman.

Thus we have been advised on the one hand to purchase guns and knives for our protection. On the other hand we have been warned that such weapons can be taken away and used against us. Still another factor that often comes into the question is the legality of the weapon. Many women have warded off assailants only to find themselves charged with carrying illegal weapons. And some women who have used weapons fatally in certain circumstances have been prosecuted for murder.

Whether or not to use a weapon must be an individua decision.. There are advantages and disadvantages that will vary from person to person and circum-stance to circumstance. No one can make your decision for you. If you are considering the purchase of a weapon, there are some important questions you will want to take into account. One is the legality of the weapon you are con-templating. Laws vary from state to state and city to city. Call the local police department to check on the weapon you are considering. It is frustrating and humiliating to find that the officer who responds to your call is more interested in you and your crime than in the rapist who attacked you.

Your level of expertise with any weapon you choose should be such that you can maintain control of it at all times. This control is important not only to make sure that the weapon cannot be taken away from you, but also so you can control the amount of damage you do to an attacker. How much you hurt him should always be *your* decision.

If you decide to rely on a weapon for self-defense, make sure that it is available at all times. It won't do you any good at the bottom of your purse or in the next room. The ability to respond without hesitation or delay is of the ut-most importance in an attack situation. Groping around for your weapon is not a particularly devastating defense.

My own personal evaluation of the above considerations is that weapons like knives and guns are not worth the risk and uncertainty that goes with them, particularly if you are relying on them as your primary means of defense. In an attack situation, however, you should use every possible technique or object that can help you defend yourself. Often the surrounding area will offer a number of objects that can be used as back-up to your defense strategy—impromptu weapons.

The objects that you might be able to use will vary with the circumstances and surroundings. One of the determining factors in the choice of weapons is the distance between you and your attacker. Distances can be divided into three groups: far, arm's length, and very close.

If an assailant is far away, perhaps across a room from you, you will want to keep him at a distance *and* drive him away. In this type of situation, objects that can be thrown are very effective. Choose something that is heavy enough to cause pain or injury, but light enough for you to throw with accuracy. If you

miss your target, you will seem weak and foolish. Larger objects can more easily be thrown on target, as long as they are not too heavy for you to move.

Throwing is a basic motor skill that many women never develop fully. If you know that you throw poorly, practice throwing balls to improve your technique and accuracy. The most forceful throwing form is one in which your leading leg opposes your throwing arm. As you throw, step out with the foot opposite the throwing arm. An overhand throw with a strong backswing will give more power to your object than an underhand or sidearm swing. Force is not the only consideration. If you don't want to alert someone that you are throwing, eliminate or cut down the backswing. Such a choice depends somewhat on the distance between you and the attacker, since eliminating the backswing may cause your weapon to fall short of its target.

Examine the objects in your home for throwing possibilities. Check the weight and size to make sure you could throw them with ease. Think about the effect each one might have on an assailant. Since it is necessary to cause at least some pain to stop an attack, pillows are not a good choice. Things that will break and possibly cut an attacker produce the greatest deterrence. The kitchen offers a particularly outstanding arsenal. And when you are outdoors, you can throw anything that you are carrying and willing to sacrifice. Depending on the circumstances of the attack, you may be able to pick up rocks or other items in the surroundings outside.

In choosing your weapons, however, do not put yourself in a poor defensive position. Always keep your attention centered on the assailant. And keep up a steady barrage until he either has fled or become incapacitated.

Large objects can be used as obstacles to keep an attacker away from you or to make it difficult for him to catch you if you're running away. Chairs, bicycles, benches, tables, just about any article of furniture, or any large, movable object can be turned over in a pursuer's path. It takes time, though, to create the obstacles. Make sure that the gain in slowing down the attacker is worth the extra time.

Large objects can also be used to secure a downed assailant. If you knock your attacker down and want to keep him there, turn the couch over on top of him. If he's unconscious, but you don't know for how long, secure him until you can get help or get away.

Another possibility for keeping an assailant at a great distance is an object that you can swing in an arc, such as a handbag on a long strap or a broom. The disadvantage in employing such a maneuver is that, as soon as you stop swinging, he can move in on you. You have to keep on swinging and hope that he goes away on his own.

In order to cause injury to an assailant you would have to move in close enough to reach him. A swinging weapon acts like a club and has the same disadvantages discussed in chapter 5. A rigid weapon, such as a pole of some sort, has more capabilities as a club than something soft on a strap. A handbag requires a large backswing, affording an assailant ample opportunity to dodge or block the blow. A pole-like weapon can be moved faster and inflict greater injury at the first blow. It can also be used with a direct jabbing motion rather than the more awkward swing.

When the attacker is within arm's reach of you, your main task is to keep him from establishing a hold on you. Secondary to this is the problem of driving him away. Irritating substances thrown into the face and eyes can momentarily confuse and stun an attacker, giving you an opportunity to follow up with a more vigorous defense or to escape. Anything you are drinking, hot or cold, can go into his face. Pepper, dirt and other powdery substances are also very effective when directed toward the eyes, as are all types of spray, from deodorant to cleansers. None of these substances has a very long reach. They must be used in fairly close range if they are to be effective. And, when used outdoors, you must have the wind with you. If you use them when an attacker is too far away, you will waste time and lose the opportunity to employ an effective technique—and you will appear weak and ineffectual. If your distance is correct, you must follow your initial defense with some maneuver that will immobilize or incapacitate him—unless he runs away first.

Sharp objects have a considerable capacity for injury, but they also present some of the same problems that knives present. If you use a kitchen knife, scissors, or some other sharp weapon, use it decisively and quickly. The great danger associated with sharp weapons sometimes causes us to hesitate to use them. Make up your mind that the situation warrants it before you reveal your intention. If you threaten an assailant with a sharp weapon, he will have a chance to prepare to fend off your blows.

When you are at arm's length from an assailant, those objects with a long reach are the best choice, unless you decide to take the risk of getting closer to him. Of course, in the heat of the struggle, you may not have a wide choice of weapons and will have to use whatever is available. Many common everyday objects can be used as a bludgeon in the case of an attacker at arm's length. Quickness and decisiveness are as important with bludgeons as they are with sharp weapons. If you hesitate, your attacker may manage to avoid your blows and regain the advantage. Choice of an object is important, too. You must pick something that will do serious damage, not a soft object like a pillow or newspaper. A lamp, skillet, heavy book, iron, and many household objects offer ample service in your defense. In your own home try to be aware of the locations of likely weapons. Test them for possible use, making sure that they are available and light enough to swing easily to target. The necessity for a backswing in bludgeon-type weapons is a drawback because the assailant will probably be

able to see what is coming. You may be able to divert his attention or time your action to coincide with his looking away from you. If you cannot offset this drawback by diversion, you will have to beat it with speed and determination.

If an assailant has already grabbed you, the distance between the two of you is so small that the use of most weapons will be ineffective. Your choice of weapons is restricted by your limited reach, and often you won't have enough room for an adequate backswing. The target area is very important in such situations. You should aim for the most vulnerable areas with weapons that do not require much of a backswing.

Sharp objects are particularly useful, since they can cause considerable pain without backswing. Bludgeon weapons are helpful if you can reach them and manage to bring them down on an attacker's head. Even a small amount

of pain should cause him to back off at least enough to give you room to employ a more effective technique. Usually in such close circumstances, hand-and-foot techniques and hold breaks are more effective than any weapon. Use the weapons only if they are within easy reach and can be moved quickly. Always continue your defense until the attacker is no longer a threat to you.

A special category of impromptu weapons are those that can be used in defense against other weapons. Knives are especially vulnerable to counter-weapons that can be used to trap them. The use of an object in defense against a knife drastically cuts down your risk of injury in the course of the struggle.

Soft, compact articles such as pillows, handbags or backpacks can skewer a knife, removing its injury potential. Hold the object in both hands and move in quickly toward the knife. It is best to hold the skewering object to one side rather than directly in front of your body. Take care that your body is out of the path of the knife in case you miss. You can move just as effectively in this manner, with much less danger to yourself.

Once the knife is skewered, direct your attention to the wielder of the knife. He must be incapacitated before he can recover the use of his weapon.

Articles of clothing, curtains, and other similar items can be used as padding for your blocking arm in a knife attack. Wrap anything handy around your arm to help protect it from cuts in using the techniques outlined in chapter 5.

The same type of article can be used to trap the knife, especially if the attacker is too far away for a skewering technique. Hold a corner of the cloth lightly in one hand. Swing it loosely in a circle; don't wave it in front of you like a bullfighter's cloak. As you move in close to the knife, trap it by swinging out in the circle, then cutting sharply to the inside with a whipping motion. Do not let go of your cloth until you are sure that the knife is no longer a threat to you. If you are able to catch it sharply enough, it will fly out of the attacker's hand. In that case, put yourself between the assailant and the knife and continue your defense, or you may be able to get to the knife before he does and remove it from the area of the struggle. If you choose to go for the knife instead of the assailant, make sure that you don't sacrifice any advantage gained in position or attention to get the knife. Even without the knife, an attacker is still a threat to you unless he runs away.

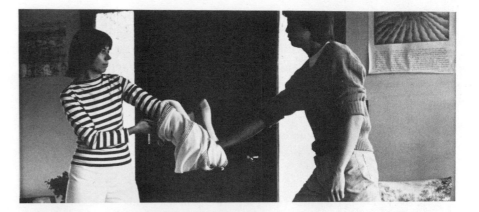

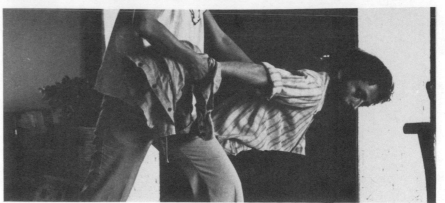

If your whipping motion did not cause the assailant to lose the knife, it will wrap around the knife and his hand, binding them together. If this happens, move in close to him, without letting go of your cloth. As soon as you can, grasp his knife-holding arm and don't let go until you have removed the knife. (Most of the arm locks in chapter 4 are easily adapted to the disarming of an opponent.) Take care to move your body to the side and out of danger from the knife while you are taking it out of his hand. In some situations you may have to use a counterattack to stun or knock him out before you can disarm him. If this is the case, remember not to let his knife hand out of your control.

Multiple Assailants

1. Do not let the search for a weapon take your attention away from the positions and movements of the attackers.

2. If one attacker is farther away than another, use an obstacle or throwing weapon to keep the distant one at bay while you deal with the close one.

3. Do not start toward one attacker with a weapon when another is in a position to disarm you.

4. Use obstacles to deny access to you by distant attackers while you either escape or defend yourself against closer assailants.

5. A swinging object can be used to keep more than one attacker at a time away from you. Don't let one of them get out of your sight, though, or he could possibly break through the arc while you are unaware of his movements.

Chapter 7
Special Situations

The techniques presented in the preceding chapters are designed for use in a variety of situations. Most of them assume a certain amount of freedom of movement on your part. There are special situations where circumstances that restrict your movement will necessarily inhibit your choice of techniques. Four are discussed here: inside a car, on the floor or ground, in bed, and on stairs.

As soon as you find yourself under attack in difficult circumstances, your first task will be to consider the possible responses at your disposal. If your hands are pinned, use your feet. Don't waste energy and time on a difficult or unlikely response; rely on whatever is easiest. Take into account any particular dangers involved due to the circumstances and plan your defense accordingly.

Inside a Car

One of the most common situations that demands special attention is when you are inside a car with an assailant. Many self-defense experts dismiss this danger by advising women not to hitchhike. Although hitchhiking can be dangerous, I believe that whether or not to hitchhike is a woman's own decision. And it is certainly not the only way a woman ends up in a car with a po-

tential rapist. Someone may hide in your car while it is parked. He may enter your car as you are stopped at a stoplight or caught in slow-moving traffic. You may be forced into his car and ordered to drive someplace. Car pools, dates, and fathers driving babysitters home are all possibly dangerous situations. Regardless of whether you hitchhike, you must be prepared for the possibility of defending yourself in an automobile.

Obviously most of us can't completely avoid being alone in a car with a man, known or unknown. But you should be able to defend yourself if the necessity arises. One of the most important things about cars is that they take you away from relatively safe territory to possibly more hazardous places. Whenever an attacker wants to move you from one place to another, you can bet the other place will be more to his advantage. Consequently, in cases where you are being forced into a car, it is often a good choice to make your stand right there, rather than risk being transported. You should try to get yourself out of the situation before you are hopelessly far away from help and safety.

The interior of a car is an extremely difficult environment in which to defend yourself. In the confined area it is hard to maneuver; your legs are

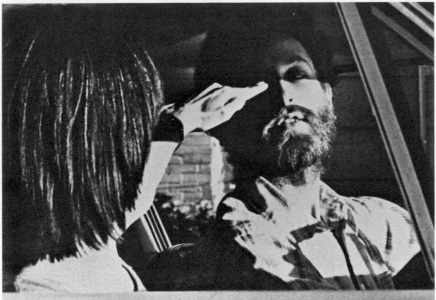

cramped and practically useless. The situation is complicated even more if the attacker is in control of the moving car. If you hurt or disable him, you have the problem of gaining control of the car before it crashes.

The great amount of risk involved with defense inside cars dictates increased caution, or better, *precaution*. You should always lock your car even if you only leave it for a few minutes. Always check for someone hiding when you get in, even though it was locked.

Hitchhikers should consider carefully the decision to hitchhike. If you do hitchhike, choose your rides cautiously and stay alert and wary at all times.

Once you are in a car with an assailant, your problems will fall into two groups: getting out of the car and escaping, and fighting with him inside the car. If you are driving, getting out of the car is a relatively easy task. A minor accident, stop sign, or heavily populated area can give you a chance to jump out if you are quick. If you have decided to abandon the car to the assailant, don't hesitate while getting out—don't turn off the ignition, put on the emergency brake, or do any of the normally habitual things one does on leaving a car. Just jump out and run. Even if he follows you, you will have an easier time fighting in the street than in the car.

Whenever you are in a strange car with a strange man, familiarize yourself with your surroundings and position yourself in the best possible way for defense. Figure out how the door opens. Avoid putting on a seat belt, but if you are forced to fasten it, make sure you know how to get out of it. Roll down the window if you can. Seat yourself sideways so you can see what he is doing. From a sideways position you can also draw your feet up so that you can use them to keep him away from you. Keep one hand close to the door handle. Notice whether the car is automatic or standard shift, where the ignition is, and other details that might help you fight.

(If you are with a stranger, you may be able to get his name or some clue to his identity from objects inside the car. If there is a possibility that you might prosecute, try to leave something of yours in the car to help establish later that he did abduct you.)

The main problem in getting out of a car is finding or making an opportunity. Within a town or city, traffic more easily affords an opportunity for escape than on an open road or freeway. When someone else is driving, it is difficult to make your own opportunity to escape. You will have to be ready to jump out immediately whenever the opportunity arises. At the same time you must not appear to be thinking about escape, so your captor won't take any precautions against it. Depending on your evaluation of his state of mind, you may be able to trick him into stopping.

If there is no opportunity to escape, or if you decide that it is imperative to take control immediately, you may have to fight inside the car. The confined area severely restricts your movement and choice of techniques. You will have to begin the struggle while the car is on a relatively safe path. You may be able to stop suddenly and launch your defense while your attacker is recovering from the jolt. If he is driving, you may have to try to stun him and then stop the car.

If he is driving and the car is in motion, your first technique should be just enough to make him stop the car. However, you don't want to knock him out at the wheel unless you are reasonably certain of being able to control the car. At the same time don't use a defense so mild that he will be merely irritated and more cautious.

Basic Punch

The basic karate punch can be used with considerable effectiveness, although it is less effective inside a car than it is outside a car where there are no restrictions to your movement. Your power will come solely from your arm and shoulder, since in most cases you will not be able to put your weight behind the punch. If you are in the passenger seat, you will be able to use either your right hand or your left. If you are driving, only your right will be in a position to strike—and it will be from an awkward position at that. You must, in any case, direct your punch to one of the most vulnerable targets—probably the head.

Strike to Eyes

Drivers who can't see generally panic and stop the car. A strike to the eyes is an excellent choice if the car is going slowly and the driver will be able to stop before doing much damage. It is also a good choice if the assailant is not the driver, or if the car is stopped. The strike to the eyes usually requires that you be closer to the attacker than does the punch. Moving your hand straight into the eyes may be difficult in the confines of the car. A better motion is a circular one with the open hand, so that the tips of the fingers go into the one eye that you can easily reach.

Elbow Techniques

Most of the elbow techniques presented in chapter 2 are adaptable for use inside a car. They are weakened, though, when your range of motion is restricted. It is important to aim for tender points like the nose, mouth, and chin. The elbow techniques, developed for fighting at close range, are most effective when you are very close to the attacker.

Back Fist Strike

The back fist strike can deliver power from farther away than any of the above techniques, although it is relatively weak compared to the basic punch and must be directed to the extremely tender areas.

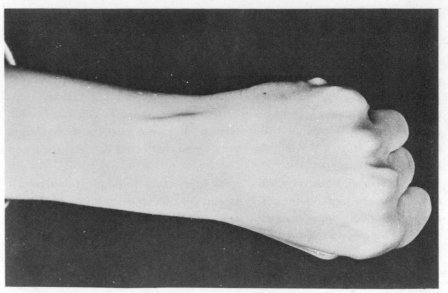

To practice the back fist strike, stand comfortably or sit in a chair. Hold your right fist just in front of your right shoulder, palm facing in to your shoulder. Your arm is bent at the elbow, which points directly to your right side. Your arm is parallel to the floor. To execute the strike, fling your fist out to the right side, locking your elbow as your arm reaches full extension. You will be striking with the knuckles of the back of your fist. Pull your fist quickly back in to its position in front of your shoulder. Practice with your right and left hands.

The back fist strike can be used from a number of different positions and thus is good for use inside a car. It can reach someone next to you and also someone in the back seat. The power of the back fist strike depends on the snap of your arm and the choice of targets. Its inherent weakness makes it a poor choice in situations where a more powerful blow can be employed.

Foot Techniques

If you are able to draw up your feet, move your body into a sideways position, and brace yourself against the door; you may be able to kick your assailant in the face. Use the same basic motion as the front kick. Your feet will give you the longest reach, but unless you can mask your preparatory moves, your feet will be slow and clumsy—and probably ineffectual.

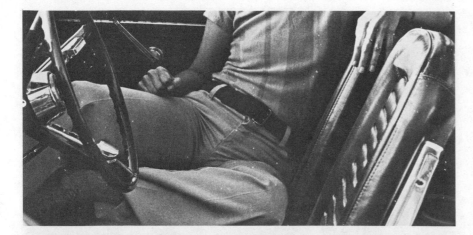

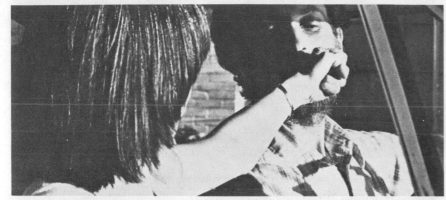

On the Floor

Another awkward position from which to defend yourself is the floor or ground. Usually, the first move an assailant attempts is to throw you down. Try to avoid falling by initiating a forceful defense before he has a chance to get you down. If you *are* thrown down, don't give up. It is more difficult to fight from a downed position, but it is possible.

The least advantageous position on the ground is face down, so try to land so you can see and also keep the use of your arms and legs. If you do wind up prone, turn over as quickly as you can. Of primary importance when you're down is to prevent an attacker from keeping you there. Use your feet to keep an attacker away from you until you can get up. It is best to stabilize yourself with your arms and one leg and use the other leg to kick out at him. Your kicks

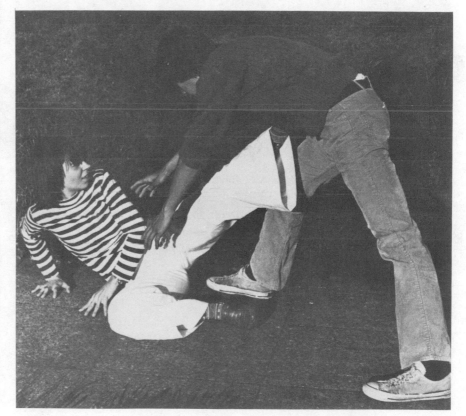

should be rapid and numerous. Aim for his knees and shins. Do not let him grab your leg.

If he comes close to you in an attempt to pin you on the ground, he will have to bend over to reach you. As he bends, his balance will be off, and you will have your best opportunity to strike out at him. In this instance go for power and a tender spot.

Basic Punch

Punching is difficult from the floor or ground because your position keeps you from pulling your elbow back behind you. If you manage to raise your torso enough to gain room to maneuver, you will be able to punch, but your blow will be relatively weak since your base is unstable. By pulling your elbow out to the side, you can punch in a sideways direction, catching the attacker's temple, ear, nose, jaw, or mouth. A sideways punch will probably have more power than a direct one, depending on the position of you and your attacker.

Back Fist Strike

A back fist strike can be more effective from the ground than a punch. It relies on the snap of the arm and doesn't require as much of a stable base as the punch. Remember that its power is small compared to other techniques. Another disadvantage is its limited reach.

A back fist from the ground is most valuable in situations where the assailant is bending over, which brings his head into range, or in cases where your legs are pinned or otherwise made useless. The back fist should always be followed by escape or a continuing vigorous defense.

niques described in chapter 2 are effective. None requires more room than you will have on the ground. It is especially important when you are down to follow those techniques by more forceful blows and a shifting to a position advantageous to you.

In Bed

It is not uncommon for a woman to awaken in the middle of the night to find an assailant standing next to her bed. Those of us who live in cities, especially in busy apartment complexes, are often not very sensitive to the noise of an intruder. Students living in groups are especially prone to ignore sounds of people coming and going at various times. And many of us, upon hearing strange noises, remain in bed, terrified, instead of getting up to investigate. I suppose those who wait in bed are hoping that the noise is just a burglar who will leave without doing any bodily harm. In my opinion that's too big a risk for a woman to take. She should at least get out of bed and wait behind the door. Defense from under the covers on a bed is extremely difficult.

If you are caught in bed, the covers will be the immediate problem. As soon as you perceive danger, throw off the covers. If that is impossible, try to at least get your arms out. You must get yourself unencumbered at the first opportunity.

I have heard of rapists who, upon surprising a woman in bed, dragged her out of the bed and into another room to rape her. If he's attempting such a move, it will probably be to your advantage to go with him, at least to the point where you are out of bed. You will have a better chance of fighting back once you're free of the entanglement of the covers.

Even if he does not intend to move you to another room, there is a good chance that the assailant will throw off the covers himself. Particularly where rape is the object, the covers are as much a hindrance to him as they are to you. If he tries to rip off the covers, your first reaction will probably be to resist, to keep yourself covered. Don't let modesty get the best of common sense here; get rid of the covers and then deal with him. He won't be able to see much if you knock him out.

As soon as you are free of the covers, you can employ any of the techniques just described for when you are on the ground. At the first opportunity, get out of bed and continue your defense from a more advantageous position.

Elbow and Knee Techniques

The elbow techniques have the shortest reach of all the moves presented in this book. By the time an attacker comes into range of an elbow technique, he usually has already secured your arms. There is a point, nevertheless, just as he comes in and reaches to pin your arms, when you are free to use your elbows. The front, side, and upward elbow strikes are most likely to be useful in such cases. There is also a chance that he might not pin your arms, or that at some point in the struggle he might release them, giving you an opportunity to strike. At this range your knee should go into his groin with as much force as you can muster at the first opportunity.

When his body is pressed on top of yours, all the close-in fighting tech-

Stairs

Stairs present special defensive problems since they increase the hazard of losing your balance as well as restrict your movement. Targets also shift from the normal range, since it is unlikely that attacker and victim will be on the same level. If you can delay a struggle until you move to a safer place, that should be your first choice. Whenever only one assailant is involved, it should be fairly easy to move—though perhaps not in the direction you were originally going—to a level space before you are forced to fight. If you are caught on the stairs, don't forget an attacker will have the same problems you have.

The first task on the stairs is to secure your balance. If your shoes are a hindrance, kick them off. Back against a wall, if possible, and hold on to the railing if there is one. If the stairs are open on one side, it is important to move to the protected side. If they are open on both sides, each side will be equally hazardous, so try to stay in the middle and don't put yourself in a position from which you might fall or be pushed over the side.

If you grasp a railing on the wall side with both hands behind you, you will still have both feet free to kick in any direction. If there is no railing, put your back against the wall for support and keep your hands close to the wall for balance.

Immediately examine the stairs to determine potential hazards and avenues of escape. Try to move so that you keep the attacker always at a disadvantage. It is best to keep him at a level lower than yours at all times. If he is higher than you, the only vulnerable targets you will have access to are his groin and knees. In addition your techniques will have to be thrown against gravity, and you will have an unstable base. These factors will weaken your techniques.

On the other hand, if the assailant is lower than you are, you will be able to reach his head and its vulnerable spots. Gravity will not only give your techniques more power, but will probably draw your attacker down once his balance is disrupted. Also, he will fall away from you, rather than toward you. If he gets up, he will have to run up the stairs to chase you.

To keep your balance, you will have to adjust your stance when fighting on stairs. It is important to keep both feet on the same step, which necessitates a short, relatively narrow stance. If you are against a wall, brace one foot (your right, if you are right-handed) against the wall and place the other ahead of it. Keep your feet away from the edge of the steps so you don't risk slipping.

Basic Kick

If you are holding on to a railing, the front kick can be used in modification to strike in any direction. This kick gives you the longest reach and most power. If an attacker is standing below you, don't hesitate to kick for targets on his head.

Basic Punch

The punch is more effective in cases where the assailant is on the lower level or on the same level as you. This position enables you to strike his head without endangering yourself much. If you must use the punch to an attacker above you, the technique will be weakened and the targets limited to the groin or knee.

Elbow and Knee Techniques

If an attacker is close enough to you so you can use an elbow or knee technique, he is also close enough to throw you down the stairs. Consequently, you must act without hesitation, and your defense must be strong and continue until you are out of danger. It is of the utmost importance in such cases to aim your blows for the targets on the head and the groin. As soon as you strike, push your assailant away from you and continue fighting until you are safe.

It is impossible to cover all the difficult situations you may encounter. In addition they are always more difficult to fight in than an environment that presents no special problems. Hence you should always try to avoid hazardous situations. Vigilance and preparedness are extremely important. Try to start reacting early enough to choose your own spot for defense.

If you ever find yourself in a difficult position, moreover, remain calm and figure out how to adapt the tools you already have to fit the situation. The techniques displayed in this book have been chosen for adaptability. If you have mastered them, and if you have spent a little time thinking about what to do in various situations, you should be able to apply the proper defense if the occasion ever arises.

Multiple Attackers

The problems of the special situations are multiplied if the number of attackers is greater than one. Consequently, the first principle in fending off multiple attackers in such situations is to try to maneuver the group so that you are in the best possible position.

1. In a car, strike nondrivers before drivers, if reach and position permit. The ones who aren't driving have nothing to hamper their attacking you once you have launched your defense, but the driver has to worry about keeping the car on the road.

2. In bed, or on the ground, it is usually best to strike the one nearest you first.

3. From the ground, if one attacker is balanced and another is slightly off-balance, move first against the off-balance one.

4. On stairs, if everything else is equal, move first against the attacker standing above you.

5. Use the restrictions of whatever situation you find yourself in against the group of attackers. Make them fall over one another down the stairs. Use one as a shield against another in close quarters.

PROBLEM 7:1—Inside a car, there is a driver; you are in the passenger seat, and an assailant is in the back seat on the right hand side. What can you do?

PROBLEM 7:2—You are in bed. One attacker stands next to the bed; the other is near the foot of the bed. What can you do?

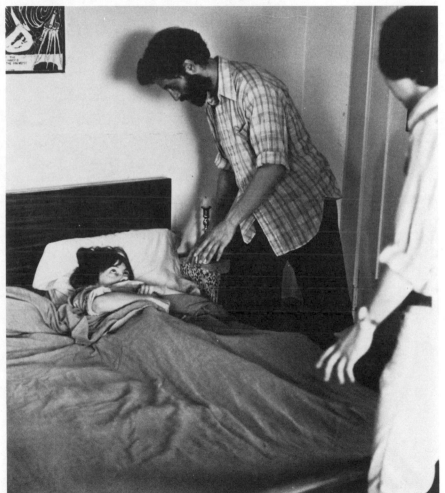

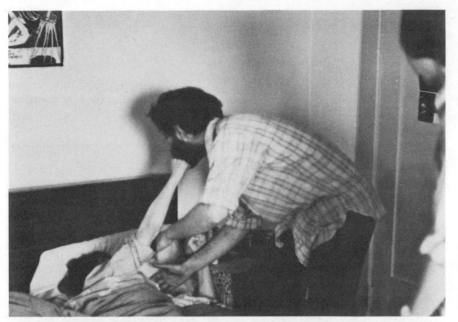

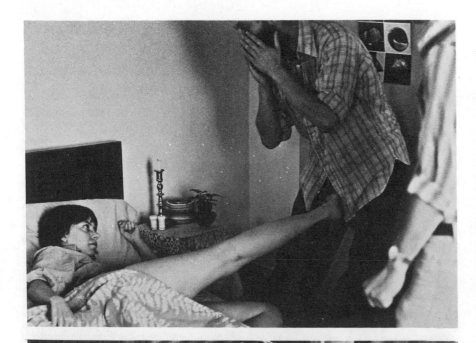

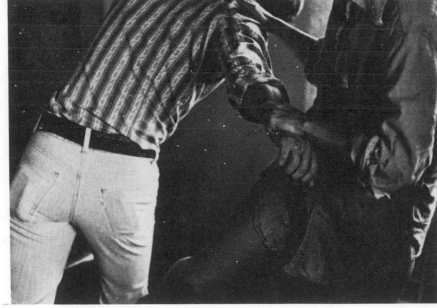

PROBLEM 7:3—You are on a stairway. One attacker is above you; one is below. What can you do?

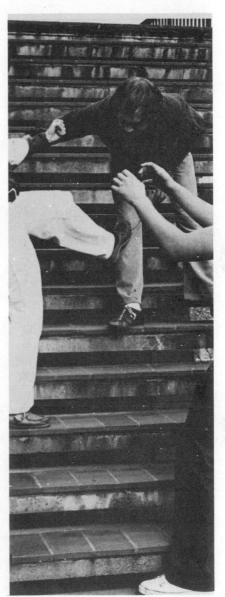

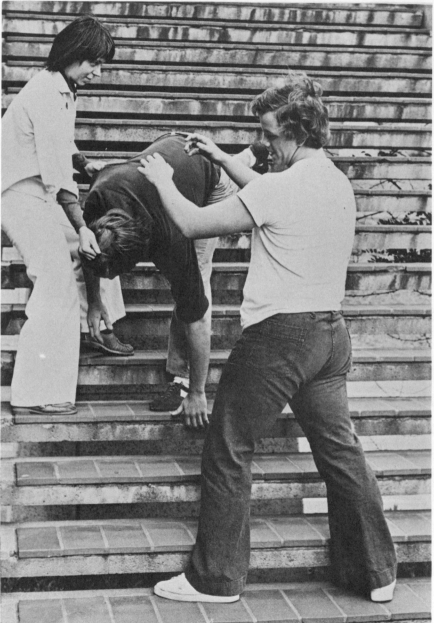

Chapter 8
Staying in Shape

The better your physical condition, the more effectively you will be able to apply your knowledge if it ever becomes necessary. Most of you will not become top-notch athletes in the interest of self-defense, but everyone should try to keep in moderately good shape for general health reasons as well as for self-defense. This chapter is not a comprehensive conditioning program for the average woman. That is something you can get from a book that deals specifically with that particular topic.

But since there are so many different programs available and some are confusing to the lay person, this chapter contains general guidelines by which to build an individual program. The major facets important to the construction of a well-rounded program are explained so that you can make sure you include the basics in your program. Specific exercises necessary to good execution of the techniques presented in this book are included, along with special problems of women that are often overlooked in other books.

Any conditioning program should be planned to develop three major objectives: flexibility, strength, and endurance. Good flexibility enhances your ability to move with speed and balance. Your muscles work more efficiently when opposing muscle groups are well balanced. Opposing muscles are those that perform opposite each other to move a limb in different directions. An important part of a good exercise program involves equal attention to opposing muscles.

Flexibility also depends on the action of muscles, tendons, and ligaments. A tendon is a fibrous structure that attaches muscle to bone. A ligament is a similar structure that connects bone to bone. Only muscles stretch; tendons and ligaments do not. Tendons and ligaments tear when stressed, producing strains and sprains. Consequently, your conditioning program will deal with stretching the muscles of the limbs in question, not ligaments or tendons.

Unfortunately, muscles also tear as well as stretch. Whatever exercises you are doing, avoid overstretching or tearing. A good technique is the use of slow, steady stretching movements rather than short, jerky motions. There has been long debate among exercise physiologists over methods of stretching exercises, but most now seem to favor static stretching, which involves slow, deliberate movement, over ballistic stretching, which involves short, jerky motions.

Static stretching means moving with a slow, steady movement to the point of pain, holding that position for a few seconds, and returning to the starting position. You must stretch to the point of pain, or you will not stretch the muscle past its present capabilities. To go beyond the initial point of pain, however, is to risk tearing. Jerky, bobbing motions are out of favor nowadays because they are believed to produce small tears in the muscle.

Development of muscle strength is an area in which women generally are behind men. Many women have had little opportunity to develop strength, and many have shunned its development out of a fear of becoming muscle-bound and unattractive. This is an unfounded fear, because a fundamental hormonal difference that contributes to a tendency in men to develop large bulky muscles is not present in women. Little research has been done on muscle strength in women, but the research that has been done indicates that women have the capabilities for developing as much strength as men, especially in the lower limbs. The upper body strength of most women is grossly underdeveloped, and there is a bigger gap to close there.

An increase in the size of the muscle fibers does seem to be necessary to an increase in strength. This does not mean that women who develop strength will become mannish in appearance. It is more likely that the increase in muscle size will be accompanied by a loss in body fat, resulting in firmer limbs with well-defined muscle groups.

Despite the claims of advertising, there is no easy way to develop strength. The only way to increase the strength of a muscle group is to require it to do more work than it usually does. There are two types of exercises designed to increase muscle strength: isometric and isotonic. Isometric exercises involve contracting the muscle without motion. This is done by pushing against an unmovable object or having two limbs of approximately equal strength oppose each other. The contraction is held for a certain length of time, then released, and the sequence is repeated.

In isotonic exercises the muscle moves against resistance. The most common—and effective—form of isotonic exercise is weight training. Weight training has been discouraged among women for a long time, and a stigma is attached to it despite overwhelming evidence that it works as well—and with no adverse results—for women as for men. Weight training is different from the sport of weight lifting. It is used to condition the body in overall strength. Weight lifting is a competitive sport.

A popular misconception is that many repetitions in training with small weights develops long, slender muscles and enhances flexibility. Light weights used repetitively develop muscle endurance. You get from exercise just what you put into it. If you make your muscle work a small load for a long time, you will increase its ability to work for a long time. Greater strength is developed by increasing the size of the weight. A good program should build muscle endurance and strength.

Inexpensive weight-training equipment can be purchased from department stores and sporting goods stores, or you can make sand bags for yourself. You don't need a lot of expensive equipment to stay in condition. Exercises that require you to lift part of your own body against gravity are a variation on weight training. Push-ups, sit-ups, and leg lifts are all examples of such exercises.

Endurance is the ability of the entire body to work at a high rate for an extended period of time with a minimum of fatigue. Your ability to exert yourself for an extended period of time depends on the efficiency of your circulatory and respiratory systems in getting oxygen to your muscles so they can do the work required. As in flexibility and strength conditioning, the only way to improve your endurance is to require your body to do more work than usual. The most common way to increase endurance is to engage in hard work, usually involving gross body motions (motions involving the entire body), for a long period of time. The goal is to raise your heart and respiratory rates and to sustain the higher rates for ten to fifteen minutes. Running or jogging, bicycling, swimming, and jumping rope are all activities that lend themselves well to endurance training.

Another method sometimes used for endurance is interval training, in which you engage in short periods of intense work with brief rests in between. Exertion is carried on for three to five minutes, followed by a rest period that is shorter than the work period. It is important and difficult to maintain the principle of overload—taxing your endurance—in interval training. The number of work intervals can be increased, as can be their intensity or their length. Another possibility is to shorten the rest period. The same kinds of activities that are used in prolonged training can be applied to interval training.

The amount of confusion and the conflicting statements about the nature of good exercise indicate that readers need some guidelines for planning an exercise program. If you carefully study the preceding pages, you should be able to evaluate the exercise programs that are available to you and pick one that is suited to your needs.

The remainder of this chapter contains exercises that deal specifically with body areas that need good conditioning for the proper execution of self-defense techniques.

Upper-Body Strength

Most women suffer from a lack of strength in their arms and shoulders. Recent studies show that women are approximately 50 percent weaker than men in upper-body strength, a weakness that is mainly due to conditioning—or rather, the lack of it. Most women need to increase strength in their arms and shoulders. Women's capabilities in this area have been ignored for a long time; yet strength in this area is important for the execution of the punch, elbow techniques, arm locks, and take-downs.

The best way to increase your strength is through weight training. If you are interested in weight training, get a good book (I recommend that you look for one on the DeLorme system) and experiment. The physical education sec-

tion of a local college bookstore will probably have a better selection than a sporting goods store.

Push-ups are probably the most straight-forward non-equipment exercise for the arms and shoulders. Many women are convinced that they cannot do push-ups, except for "girls' push-ups" done from the knees. It is true that push-ups are more effective for a man who carries relatively more weight in his shoulders, but they are also possible and good for women.

Women frequently have trouble with push-ups because they don't know how to do them properly. Place your hands on the floor about shoulder's width apart. (Spreading your feet apart shoulder's width will help distribute your weight evenly.) Hold your body straight and don't bend at the waist. Lower your chest toward the floor, keeping your body straight. If your elbows do not bend as you go down, you are swinging your stomach instead of lowering your chest. Go down as far as you can and then push back up. If you can't lower your chest all the way to the floor, don't worry. Work up to it gradually. Go down as far as you can and do as many push-ups as you can. Gradually work up to more and deeper push-ups.

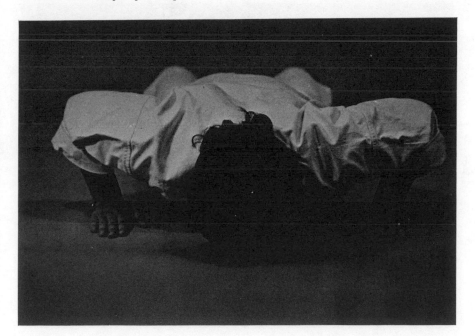

If you can't do push-ups at all, there is an exercise you can do in preparation. Stand facing a wall about two feet away from it. Place your hands on the wall, a shoulder's width apart, as if the wall were the floor in push-ups. Bend your elbows and bring your chest to the wall; then push away from the wall. As these modified push-ups become easier, move on to doing regular ones.

To increase muscle endurance in forearms and hands, hold your arms straight out in front of you. Open your hands, stretch your fingers out, and then pull them tightly into fists. A high number of repetitions are important to this exercise.

Another exercise for forearms and hands that also strengthens wrists is one that requires simple equipment that you can make yourself. Drill a hole in the middle of a piece of doweling about two feet long. Cut a piece of string long enough to reach from your chest to the floor. Tie the string to the doweling and attach a small weight to the end of the string. Hold the doweling in front of you and slowly roll the string up onto it. Then roll it slowly down to the floor again. As this exercise becomes easier, increase the weight.

Lower-Body Strength

Since many everyday activities force our legs to work, lower-body strength is relatively greater than upper-body strength. Still, there is a need in most of us to improve this area.

Strong abdominal muscles are important for kicking, as well as for other techniques presented here. Sit-ups are the easiest and most efficient exercise for strengthening these muscles. Have someone hold your feet down, or hook them under some article of furniture. Bend your knees slightly. You can either cross your arms across your chest or put your hands behind your head. Do not hold on to your legs to help yourself up. Pull your body up from a supine position forward to touch your knees to your chest.

Abdominal muscles work in several different directions. In order to strengthen them evenly, try several variations of sit-ups. Straight forward-and-back sit-ups strengthen the muscles that run straight up and down in the abdominal area. Trying to touch one shoulder to the floor and alternating sides strengthens the lateral muscles which cross the abdominal area diagonally from each side to the center. Straight-leg sit-ups increase strength in the hip rotator muscles as well as in the abdominal muscles. After you have worked up to the number of repetitions you desire, you can increase your work load by holding a heavy object behind your head as you pull yourself up.

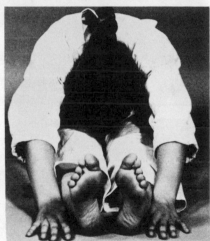

Flexibility is important to kicking, and it is one of the common problems karate students find in conditioning. Good flexibility helps you keep your balance and makes it possible for you easily to extend your kick. For the front kick the important muscles that give problems are in the backs of the legs—the hamstrings in the back of the thigh and the muscles of the calves.

To stretch the hamstrings, sit down on the floor, back straight, legs extended straight in front of you, toes together and pointing up. Extend your

hands to the front, toward your toes, or let them rest at your sides. Slowly and with steady pressure, bend at the waist as far forward as possible, or until your chest touches your thighs. Remain in this position for a few seconds; release and relax for a few seconds; then bend down again. Stretch over your legs several times; then bend down and hold that position for a count of ten.

Next, spread your feet apart as wide as you can. Still keeping your legs flat on the floor (don't let your knees bend) and your toes pointing up, lower your chest first to one knee, then to the other, slowly and with steady pressure. Repeat several times; then hold your position over each leg for a count of ten.

To stretch calf muscles, hold onto the back of a chair or the edge of a table. Place one foot close to the chair, bending the knee. Place the other foot about two and one-half or three feet behind the front one, keeping the heel placed firmly on the floor. Lean forward, bending your front knee. Stretch with a steady motion. Repeat several times; then change your position to stretch the other leg.

These supplementary exercises, plus any program you put together, should be adequate for your needs unless you have some special problems. Those who have special physical problems should consult a doctor before beginning any exercise program. Women over forty should also consult a doctor before embarking on any exercise program.

Chapter 9

Karate

Readers who have studied the foregoing chapters diligently and have learned the techniques with a certain degree of success may wonder where to go from here. You who have persevered in learning the techniques in this book have every reason to be proud of yourselves, and you probably also have an interest in pursuing your newly developed skills. At this point there is no substitute for a careful teacher—in person—who can help correct movements and broaden skills as your potential develops. Consistent and supervised training is by far the best way to maintain and sharpen your abilities. In most areas the best place to get supervised training is at a local karate school. (The term *karate* is used to encompass all the Asian martial arts, with no intention of offending anyone.)

Karate is an art based on self-defense. It also is a philosophy, a sport, a means of physical conditioning, and many other things. At the root of all these objectives, however, is self-defense. If you decide to take a formal course in karate, try everything that is presented. Don't attempt to single out the parts that seem to apply particularly to self-defense. If you give every part of the training your best effort, you will find that your progress will move steadily forward.

Choosing a good karate school is often a difficult and bewildering task. Most inexperienced people select a school on the basis of location and price. This method would be fine if karate were a more organized art. Unfortunately, there is no overall form of organization at this time and no prospect for one in the future. Consequently, novices are left to pick a school blindly out of the phone book.

Every school is different: they excel in different areas; some excel in none, but none excel in all. The pointers given here will help you find a good school by giving you a basis on which to judge your choices. They are not a check list for the best school, but rather, provide grounds for discussion with a prospective instructor.

Karate is the most popular term for a variety of forms of unarmed self-defense. In looking at a list of schools, however, you will notice a number of terms, many of which may be unfamiliar to you. Karate usually refers to the traditional Japanese art of self-defense; kung fu (or gung fu) to the Chinese art; tae-kwon-do and hapkido are Korean methods of self-defense. (I will not discuss fundamentally different arts like judo or aikido.) Within each group there are "styles," which differ from one another in varying degrees. In addition specifically American styles have grown up more recently. These usually are based more or less on one or another of the traditional Asian styles or a combination of traditional styles. All the various styles are essentially similar to one another; their differences are more obvious (and important) to experts than to novices.

Any instructor naturally thinks his or her style is best, and some of them will tell you that everybody else is wrong. Don't take anyone's word; decide for yourself. You can't tell what is best by a name, or by what an instructor says. If an instructor won't let you observe a class session, he or she is asking you to buy a product sight unseen. Most are happy to let you observe, and many are willing to let prospective students participate in a class before they sign up formally.

Since schools are unregulated by any overall or outside agency, the name of a school itself does not necessarily indicate any official certification or ties with other groups. Anyone can set up a school and name it "The Japan Karate _____," whether or not he has any ties with any group in Japan. Inclusion of the name of a state in the name of the school does not imply state approval or certification or even that the school has a statewide network. The inclusion of a phrase in advertising such as "All instructors certified by _____" is similarly meaningless. Divisions among karate groups are so great that there is no official body of certification for all schools. Each group has its own, and they can make the name as grandiose as they like.

Karate is a business. Anyone who wishes to teach full time has to make a living at it. A tireless teacher, dedicated to the art, who accepts little or no payment and works long hours to support himself or herself and spends all his or her spare time teaching people karate for free is a rarity. And that person may not be the best teacher. There is nothing wrong with a professional instructor trying to make the product sound outstanding to potential customers, but treat advertising just as you would any other professional's ads. Examine and test the product before you buy.

The qualifications of an instructor are naturally a primary concern to a student. Once again, novices usually depend upon an indication of qualification that is not necessarily reliable—rank. The meaning of rank differs from style to style. In the Chinese styles there are no formal or outwardly visible ranks such as a black belt. Everyone who is qualified as an instructor is referred to as a "master." In the Japanese and related styles, there is usually only one "master" per style, the highest ranking instructor in the style. In the styles that use the black belt as a rank, there are eight to ten degrees of black belt. In some styles promotion is rapid to the highest ranks. In others the young instructors stay in the first- to third-degree range until they gain maturity and build fairly large organizations or make some outstanding contribution to the art.

Since you can't tell by the packaging what kind of training you are likely to receive from a given instructor, concentrate on examining his work. Don't just look at the certificate of rank on his wall; watch him teach. Observe his students, who are the products of his instruction.

Finally, consider whether you want to be taught by a man or a woman. It is true that women instructors are still fairly uncommon. I do believe, however, that a man has some difficulties to overcome in teaching women that a woman does not have, so you might want to check to see if there are women instructors available in your area. In any case, insist on observing a class and discussing your needs with an instructor before you lay your money down. (Obviously, you should avoid those male instructors who pay no attention to women students. Others may make a sincere effort, but, failing to understand what the capabilities of women are, they may not be effective with women students.)

Remember that a well-rounded training program includes several things. Most good programs begin with calisthenics; the information in chapter 8 enables you to evaluate this aspect of the program. The rest of the program should emphasize equally technique and form (through basics and formal exercises) as well as free sparring, which is the practical application of all the techniques taught in karate. Specific self-defense techniques usually receive less emphasis than do the more versatile techniques. You may not see everything you are looking for in one class. At any one time an instructor may emphasize one technique over another and still maintain an overall balance. If you don't see any sparring, make a point of coming again to observe.

Students' skill in sparring also tells a lot about an instructor's teaching abilities and his or her philosophy of instruction and self-defense. In sparring, an instructor gives students a chance to put into practice the techniques they have learned, which are designed to injure opponents, without allowing any actual injury to occur. An instructor has to balance between putting a student into a situation as close to reality as possible and protecting the student from harm. If you look at a large number of schools, you will see extremes on either side. The growing popularity of "contact karate" reflects an emphasis on reality. In contact karate the participants are allowed to use the head as well as the body as a target to which they can make contact with their blows. The objective (in professional contact karate, though not necessarily in amateur "light contact") is to knock out the opponent or at least to knock him down. Safety equipment is worn on the hands and feet to minimize injury.

On the other end of the spectrum, some instructors allow no contact at all, even to the trunk of the body. Their students practice sparring with techniques that come within a fraction of an inch of touching the target and stop short. Most instructors allow their students to make medium-strength contact to the body, but none to the head. When a head is a target, these instructors use the no-contact system of having the technique come close but not touch the target. This is the system that I favor. It gives the student a chance to get used to hitting another human being, which is often a big obstacle for women. It also allows a student to be hit, removing the mystique of that experience. The trunk of the body is a lot stronger than most of us think, and it is important that women find that out through their own experience.

Another important advantage of the system of medium contact to the body with none to the head is that students learn the proper distance and timing for making actual contact. In a real situation, all they have to do is change the target, a comparatively simple task. Changing distance and timing to make contact when you're used to coming up short is much more difficult. Considering the case with which one can vary the target, I think contact to the head is an unnecessary risk.

In addition to examining a program offered by an instructor, take a look at the students. If you are observing a mixed class, notice the ratio of women to men. If there are no women, or only one or two, find out why. Talk to the women students, if possible. Look at the ranks of the students. Unless a class is specifically for a certain rank, you should see various ranks represented. Women should be distributed evenly throughout. A common distribution shows a smaller ratio of higher ranks as a consequence of the normal attrition rate. If a group is extremely bottom heavy, though, it could be a sign that instruction is poor. The good students who want to advance may be leaving to train somewhere else. Or it may be a new school that has not had time to build up an experienced group of students.

Inexperience does not necessarily mean poor instruction. In fact, new schools under young instructors are often vibrant and exciting—and you might have a chance to influence an instructor to provide an excellent program for women.

The atmosphere of each instructor's class is different. Notice the details, and try to figure out if you could easily fit in. Some instructors run very disciplined classes; some run classes informally. Some are almost militaristic in their approach to teaching; others relate more personally to the students. Try to determine if the students' needs are perceived and met by the instructor. Are the students working hard; do they seem to be enjoying themselves?

It is difficult for a novice to look at a group of karate students and tell whether their level of skill is high or low. If the school participates in local competition, you will have some frame of reference. Competition is part of the learning experience. A school that never tests its techniques in competition against other groups can never be sure that its students are performing at the highest possible level.

In competition a student has to react to the unfamiliar, and she or he has to react under pressure, both points that are important for self-defense. Actually fighting for your life in an attack situation is not like sparring in a karate school—the techniques you are faced with will be unfamiliar. And street techniques are not the same as tournament techniques, but the experience of facing the unknown is similar.

The pressure of competition is important in self-defense as well. Even when students have become comfortable with their performance of the techniques of self-defense, they ask how they can keep from "freezing" if they are ever attacked. Competition demands that the student perform under conditions of intense excitement. The excitement is not the same as the pressure of being in danger, but people react similarly to a wide variety of exciting stimuli. That's why the physiological signs of fear when you hear a strange noise in the night are similar to the feelings you have when you are being kissed by someone you love. And putting yourself in a position in which you must perform under pressure will train you to react properly if you are ever attacked. If an instructor keeps students out of competition, he or she prevents them from gaining this experience. This prevents them from testing and sharpening their skills against different styles.

On the other hand there are instructors who push competition for its own sake, rather than as a learning experience. An instructor who is primarily interested in collecting trophies will probably not give a good basic overall training program to all students. He or she is likely to concentrate on the most successful competitive students and neglect the others. Training will emphasize those techniques useful in competition, rather than emphasizing a good balance of skills. Once again, I favor the middle road.

After you have looked around and found a school that seems appropriate for you, sit down with the instructor and discuss what you want out of training. In such an interview you will be able to raise any questions that you come up with during your observation of classes. And you can find out if you will be able to satisfy your needs in the school. There is a growing trend among karate schools toward requiring students to sign contracts that bind them to pay for a specified amount of training. Before you commit yourself to six months or a year, be sure you will get what you want.

Everyone is different. What I have given you is from my own experience and reflects my own prejudice. Don't be nervous about raising questions. If there is something you don't understand about a class you have seen, give the instructor a chance to explain his philosophy. It may make as much sense to you as mine. At any rate you will be able to tell from his willingness to answer your questions how open he will be to responding to your needs. Good hunting.

Index